Award-Winning Designs for Woodturning

Award-Winning Designs for Woodturning

ALAN AND GILL BRIDGEWATER

Sterling Publishing Co., Inc.   New York

Published in 1987 by Sterling Publishing Co., Inc.
Two Park Avenue, New York, N.Y. 10016

Typeset by Latimer Trend & Company Ltd, Plymouth
Printed and bound in Great Britain at The Bath Press, Avon.

ISBN 0-8069-6538-X

Published by arrangement with Unwin Hyman Ltd.
First published in 1987 in Great Britain as
Winning Designs for Woodturning.
This edition available in the United States, Canada and the
Philippine Islands only.

Contents

List of colour plates 7

Introduction 8

The Projects

Swivel Jewel Box 25
C Ball

Box with Chained Lid 28
S Batty

Football Trophy 32
J Ambrose

Brickwork Box 35
J Ambrose

Wine Ladle 39
J Ambrose

Cup & Saucer 41
J Ambrose

Stacking Egg Cups 44
G Gilpin

Acorn Sewing Tidy 47
C Hovland

Skewed Bowl 50
I Walton

Christmas Table Centre 53
T Andrews

Coopered Jewel Box 57
A Anslow

Humpty Toy 61
K Biggs

Coin Holder 65
W Clarke

Rack of Coat Pegs 69
R Crowther

Four-colour Goblet 72
E Ede

Two-Tier Cake Stand 75
R Farley

Lighthouse Lamp 78
M Forge

Pair of Vases 82
A Franklin

Miner's Lamp 86
A Gill

Jewellery Display Tray 90
G Graham

Bowl in Mahogany and Sycamore 94
D Greenacre

Baby's Rattle 98
R Hamley

Lathe Bird 101
I Harrington

Box for Colour Slides 104
M Hold

Pen Set Holder 107
R Hopper

Owl Plaque 111
J Huckvale

Secret Trinket Box 114
N Law

Set of Thimbles 117
E Lloyd

Fruit Bowl on Pillars 121
A McVittie

Pin Cushion 124
A Parsler

Cotton Nests 128
L Piers

Checkered Edge Fruit Bowl 132
Dr P Ramsden

Pomander 135
Dr P Ramsden

Egg Stand 138
E Rumbles

Picture and Mirror Frames 141
J Rhys

Walking Stick Top 145
B Smith

Pencil Box 148
P Swabey

'Phone Table Lighter 151
K Williams

Dressing Table Set 155
C Walker-Smith

Dice Shaker 158
F Ward

List of colour plates

Fruit Bowl on Pillars (11) 9
A McVittie

Miner's lamp (86) 10
A Gill

Dressing Table Set (155) 11
C Walker-Smith

Pin Cushion (124) 12
A Parsler

Football trophy (32) 13
J Ambrose

Swivel Jewel Box (25) 14
C Ball

Stacking Egg Cups (44) 14
G Gilpin

Acorn Sewing Tidy (47) 15
C Hovland

Four-Colour Goblet (72) 16
E Ede

Cup & Saucer (41) 17
J Ambrose

'Phone Table Lighter (151) 18
K Williams

Box with Chained Lid (28) 19
S Batty

Box for Colour Slides (104) 19
M Hold

Humpty Toy (61) 20
K Biggs

Cotton Nests (128) 21
L Piers

Skewed Bowl (50) 22
I Walton

Pencil Box (148) 23
P Swabey

Dice Shaker (158) 23
F Ward

Set of Thimbles (117) 23
E Lloyd

Two-Tier Cake Stand (75) 24
R Farley

INTRODUCTION

The 40 projects in this book are the result of a competition arranged by the publishers and Practical Woodworking Magazine which was announced in the March 1986 edition of the magazine. The response was excellent, not only in terms of the number of entrants but in terms of the extremely high standard of the contributions themselves. A panel of judges spent an interesting time in the summer trying to narrow down the winning projects—WINNING DESIGNS IN WOODTURNING is the outcome of this difficult choice.

The projects are of a varied nature coming from wide ranging places and revealing different interests and techniques. Because of this they will appeal to a broad section of craftsmen requiring the enthusiasm of the beginner or the skill of a more experienced craftsmen.

With technical advice from the original creators, the projects have been clearly laid out to facilitate working. Diagrams and working drawings, accompanied by photographs and unambiguous instructions can be easily followed. However, this book acts more importantly as a new source of inspiration to encourage inventiveness rather than a rigidly defined set of instructions to be closely adhered to. Each design can be adapted not only to your particular lathe and tools but also to your choice of timber and personal taste.

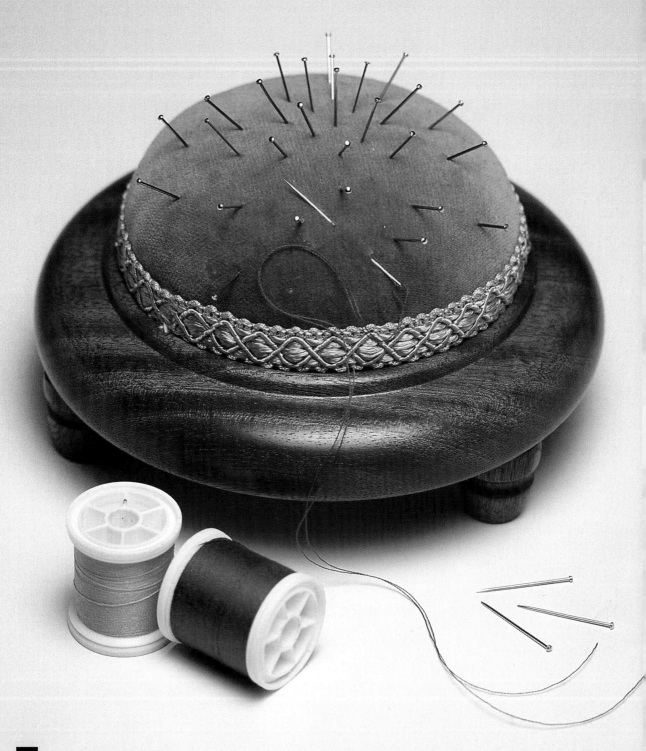

24

SWIVEL JEWEL BOX

Charles Edward Ball

Charles has always been interested in woodturning, and yet somehow, he has never quite managed to spend as much time as he would like getting to grips with the subtleties of the craft. Trained as a plumber, he taught related subjects at evening classes, and then, after building his own house, he became a self employed builder. Laterly he helped his wife convert an old house into a small hotel, and went on to help her run it. Having decided that the time was right to become involved in a bit of serious woodturning, he then repaired an old lathe, set up his workshop and generally sorted out his equipment. He worked on the lathe just long enough to realize that he needed a bit of tuition, and he has promised himself just that.

As for the project, he has doodled out many ideas for various competitions, but this is the first time he has actually worked an idea through and entered the completed project. To Charles the competition brief, as set out by Bell and Hyman/Practical Woodworking, seemed just too good to miss. At last, after years of playing around with woodturning ideas, he could put his design workouts through their paces, and Charles went on, as we all now know, to turn off a winner.

LATHE TYPE
A twenty year old Myford 8.

TOOLS AND MATERIALS
A good selection of turning tools
gouge
parting tool
scraper
bandsaw
dovetail saw
plane
workout paper
callipers
hand drill and bit
hammer
glue
pins
wax
and all the usual workshop tools

WOODS
For this project you need a quantity of red padauk for the base and spine and sycamore for the trays. Note: upon consideration, Charles, might also have used African blackwood for the base and the spine, and red mahogany for the trays.

What to do

1 Have a look at the photograph on page 14 and the working drawings, and see how although at first sight this project looks very complicated, it has been achieved quite simply by gluing 1 in thick sycamore layers together at an angle to the axis, rather than at right angles. Note also, how the initial assembly has been built up using the traditional low-tech glue and paper method.

2 When you have studied the project in detail, and have considered all the technique and design implications, build up the sycamore and waste assembly, using glue and pins. Note: place the clipped-head pins at points where the wood will later be turned out.

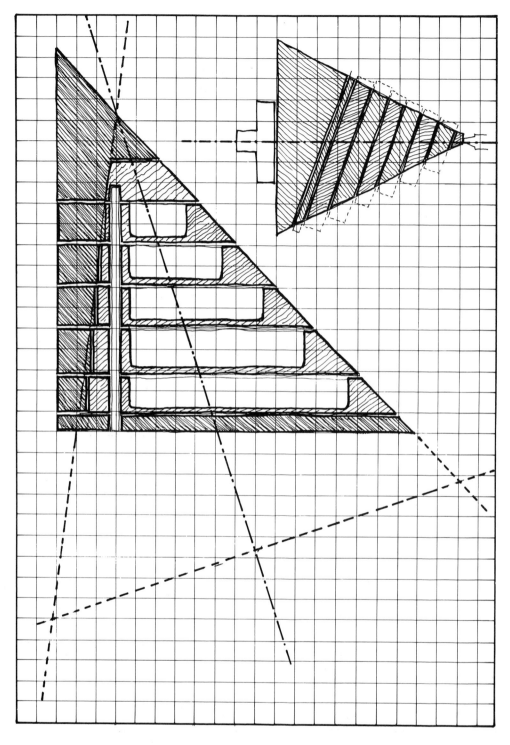

1 Working drawings. The scale is 2 grid squares to 1 in. See how the five tray blanks and the base are inititially glued and pinned. Note the waste at the turning points. Start by turning a true cone, then ease the various layers apart, remove the lathe waste/blocks, and turn each of the tray recesses.

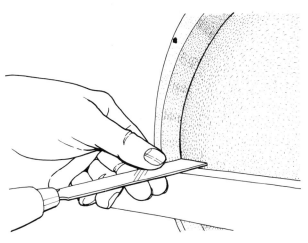

2 Mount each tray on a face plate, and turn out a recess to the maximum diameter.

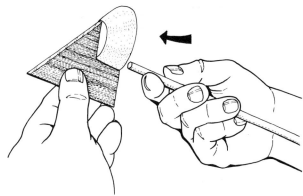

4 Start the assembly by gluing the pivotal dowel into the sycamore top cover.

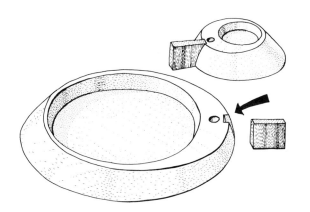

3 Work, fit, glue and position each of the spines so that the grain runs smoothly from the base to the peak. See how each spinal vertebra is let into its tray, and note the placing of the pivot hole.

5 Take the trays, a piece at a time, (note the need for recesses of maximum diameter), then mount them on a face plate and turn out to a good finish.

6 Now take the wood for the spine and cut out and fix the various parts so that the grain runs smoothly from base to peak.

7 When all the parts have been worked, start the assembly by gluing the dowel into the top sycamore cover.

8 Slide on the stack of trays and washer spacers, place and position the base and then fix the dowel to the base with either a screw, or a slot and wedge.

3 Once the tray, base and waste assembly has been put together and mounted securely between a face plate and the tailstock, then use the tools of your choice to turn off a true cone. It can be turned on an end face plate with care if the lathe centre is insufficient.

4 Take the cone to a good size and finish then remove the top and bottom waste. Drill the hole for the pivot to ensure perfect line up of holes and then carefully separate the various layers.

Afterthoughts and modifications

Although Charles considers that this project requires two contrasting timbers, it might also be successfully worked in one timber.

When you are building up the pre-lathe assembly, and reinforcing the glue-and-paper laminations with pins, make sure that the pins are either located at points which will not be seen, or at waste wood points.

Note the need for a small piece of waste at the top of the cone.

BOX WITH CHAINED LID

Stuart Batty

Stuart started woodturning when he was about twelve years old. Not for him ten minute sessions on a school lathe with a bit of rough wood and a blunt gouge, he was taught at home by his father who is a skilled and experienced woodturner. While Stuart was still at school his father started his own business selling Coronet lathes, teaching woodturning and making private commissions. And so it was, lucky lad, that by the time he was sixteen he was well on the way to being a confident and experienced woodturner in his own right. When he left school he spent a couple of years by his father's side until he went his own way and started working for a well known woodturning suppliers where he now teaches and demonstrates.

In terms of hobbies, Stuart likes nothing better than to be in his workshop, at his lathe, experimenting and turning new forms. He sells much of his work at local galleries which helps to pay for tools and materials. When it comes to designing, naturally he puts a great deal of time and thought into possible projects but his best and most successful designs seem to spring out of sudden notions or are inspired by the wood itself. As to what inspired Stuart to make this particular project – the idea came to him when he remembered that his girlfriend's birthday was fast approaching and immediately he knew that he wanted to make a jewellery box.

LATHE
Coronet major and a selection of chucks and face plates.

TOOLS AND MATERIALS
drill chuck
saw toothe bit
$\frac{1}{8}$ in parting tool
1 in skew chisel
$\frac{1}{4}$ in gouge
callipers
small saw
graded glass papers
2 wooden 'V' blocks
wax
usual small tools

WOODS
Small cylindrical blank of Honduras rosewood, a piece about $6\frac{1}{2}$ ins long and $2\frac{3}{4}$ ins plus in diameter. You will also need four spills of ebony veneer.

What to do
1 Take a look at the working drawings, details and photographs on page 19 and notice how the qualities of the rosewood are accentuated by this beautifully simple little box. See how the cylinder has been sawn along the hinge line and how four delicate ebony veneers/spills have been used to make up the kerf loss.

2 Mount your rosewood securely between centres, turn to round, and then turn and part down both ends so as to allow for mounting in a 2 in diameter spigot collet.

3 This done, part in $\frac{1}{2}$ in from the spigot ends

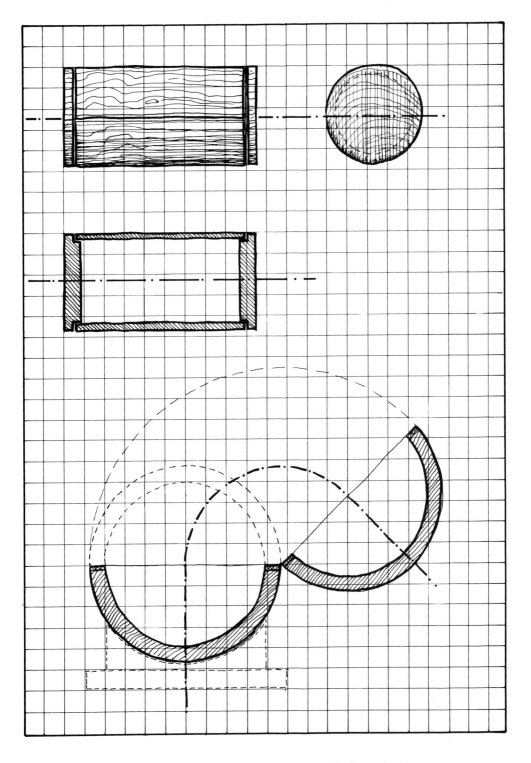

1 Working drawings. Top: the scale is 2 grid squares to 1 in. Bottom: the scale is 4 grid squares to 1 in. See how the cylinder is sawn in half and hinged along its length, and note also, in the section, how the kerf loss has been made-good with thin spills of ebony veneer.

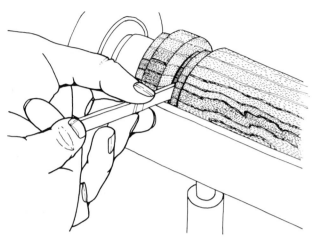

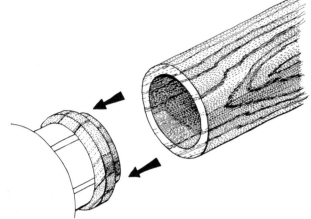

2 With the wood secured between centres, turn down the ends of the box to allow for 2 in spigot mounting, establish the thickness of the end caps, then, on the end of the box nearest the headstock, turn down a 2 in diameter spigot.

4 Piece at a time, mount the ends of the box in a spigot chuck, and turn down a 2 in diameter, $\frac{3}{16}$ in long stepped spigot. Work the wood little-by-little, and keep checking for a good fit.

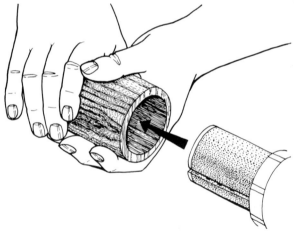

3 Cover a scrapwood chuck with sandpaper, and clean up the inside of the cylinder. Be careful not to 'rock' the box and aim to keep the edges clean cut and square.

and then at the end nearest the headstock, part in again to allow for another spigot mounting.

4 When you have checked that all is well, part off both spigot ends so that you have three pieces of wood—the two spigotted ends and the $4\frac{1}{2}$ in long centre piece.

5 Take the centre piece, mount its spigotted end in the chuck and bore in with a 2 in diameter sawtooth machine bit to a depth of about $2\frac{1}{2}$–3 ins.

6 Reverse the wood, mounting it on a wooden chuck, then bore in from the other end to complete the cylinder.

7 When the cylinder has been smoothly worked, make a sandpaper covered chuck, and clean up the inside of the tube.

8 A piece at a time, take the two box ends, mount them on the spigot chuck, and turn them down so that at about 2 in diameter, they fit in and cap off the ends of the cylinder.

9 Mount the main cylinder on the lathe, then use one of the end plugs to cap off and turn the end down until it is about $\frac{1}{4}$ in thick. Do this with both ends.

10 Now set the central section of the box on the workbench so that the choice grain is uppermost, and decide where to cut the cylinder in half.

11 Set the $4\frac{1}{2}$ in long cylinder up on two wooden V-blocks, then use a hand saw to halve it along its length.

12 Calculate the thickness of the saw cut/kerf, then veneer the four cut edges with the ebony spills, to make up the circumference loss. Rub the edges down to a good size and finish.

13 Take the two ends and the bottom half of the split cylinder, match up the grain and then glue and clamp up.

14 Finally, pivot the lid to the base with pins or hinges, mount the box on a stand/plinth, then take the wood to a good polished and waxed finish.

Afterthoughts and modifications

This project has been worked on a spigot and a wooden chuck, but you can of course modify the approach and use, say, a jawed chuck, or even a chuck with expanding collet.

If you decide to have the box hinged, rather than pin-pivoted, then round the back edge of the lid so that it doesn't catch the base.

Take the box to a polished and waxed finish after gluing, then you won't have problems with glue rejection.

When you are cutting the box in half, it is best not to use a circular saw, use a hand saw or a bandsaw.

If the veneered edges are too thick, the box will be slightly oval in section, with this problem in mind, rub the edges of the box halves down on a flat surface.

FOOTBALL TROPHY

John Ambrose
(who also designed the next three items)

John loves woodturning because he can rapidly produce beautiful articles from numerous types of timber. He derives great pleasure from collecting and converting timber from various sources, then anticipating colour and grain patterns and selecting for natural shape and defects. He remembers reading somewhere, 'Wood is where you find it'.

John was brought up in a family building business and his earliest memories are of delving into a chest full of tools and wading through a workshop that was knee deep in fine aromatic shavings. Subsequently trained as a joiner, it wasn't until about 1948, when he saw a friend working on a home made lathe, that he decided that woodturning was for him. John has a workshop and timber store at home. Timber is collected from various sources, it is generally fresh felled, or, if the project demands, kiln dried timber is bought in. As to wood types, he simply sees what is available, and carries on from there.

With regards to design, John's work is largely shaped by its purpose; it is either functional or decorative. However, before he removes a project from the lathe, he is always guided by what is most pleasing to the eye if it doesn't interfere with the usage. This particular project was inspired by mathematical construction, and was made for a retiring President of Ely Football Club. Currently, John owns a gallery near Ely Cathedral, sells his own work, gives demonstrations to local societies and makes commissioned projects.

LATHE TYPE
A 1948/49 Myford ML8, with a $\frac{1}{3}$ HP motor, and also a Dominion pattern-making lathe with a 2 HP motor and a 24 in swing.

TOOLS AND MATERIALS
selection of gouges, chisels and scrapers (some home made from a high speed cutter bar)
bandsaw
angle bed, fine blade circular saw
compass
pencil
measure
workout paper
protractor
callipers
glass fibre matt and resin
car body filler paste
shellac
beeswax
and all the usual workshop items

WOODS
African walnut for the hexagons and pentagons, small scraps of sycamore for the joints and a fairly large baulk of wood for the former/mould, (see the working drawings).

What to do

1 First take a look at the working drawings and details, notice that the project is made up from 20 hexagons and 12 pentagons, all with $1\frac{1}{2}$ in sides. Note you will need to turn off a perfect hemispherical recessed former/mould.

2 When you've come to grips with all the complexities of the project, sit back with your workout paper, a measure and a pencil, and

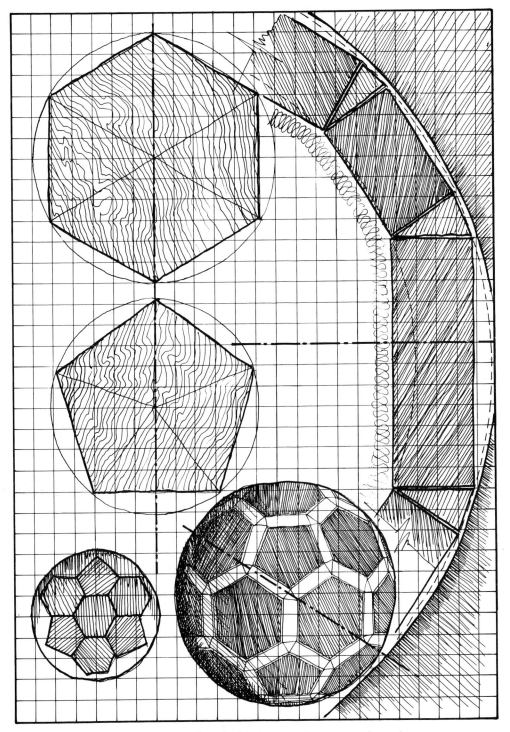

1 Working drawings. The scale of the hexagon and pentagon templates and the section, is 4 grid squares to 1 in (the small plan and the ball image are not to scale). See how the regular polygons fit together to cover the concave surface and note how the outer surface of the half-ball needs to be packed out with triangular-section filler pieces.

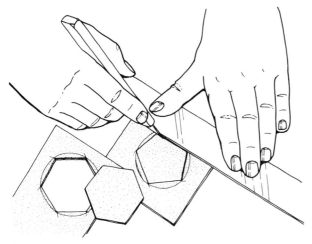

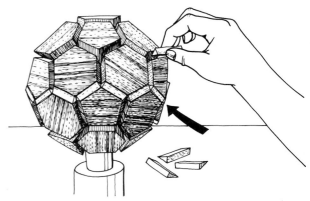

2 Using a compass and a protractor, make two accurate cardboard templates, both the pentagon and the hexagon need to have straight edges that measure 1½ins.

4 Once you have glued the two half-balls together, take the two sizes of triangular filler pieces and carefully work the outer surface of the ball. Note: the little triangular intersections need to be worked at a later stage.

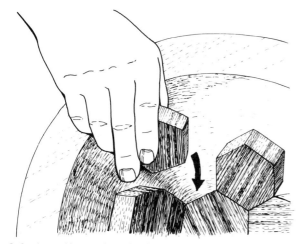

3 Set the mould out on the worksurface, then, starting with a hexagon in the centre, build up the curve of the half-ball, if necessary trim and adjust edges to fit.

5 Mount the baulk of wood on a large face plate and turn off a smooth sided bowl-profiled former.

6 Set the former on the worksurface and, starting with a hexagon in the centre, build up the curve of the half-ball.

7 When you have achieved a well set out half-ball, and you are sure all the edges are touching, smear a little car body paste over the joints, and then line the whole ball with fibreglass matting and resin.

8 When the resin has cured, lift out the first half-ball and then repeat the process and make the second half-ball.

9 Glue the two half-balls together then fill in all the wedge section joints with strips of carefully cut sycamore.

10 Glue in a temporary or permanent chuck shaft, wait for the glue to dry and then mount the whole work on the lathe.

11 Now carefully set about turning down the ball. When it is nearly finished, plug the little triangular intersections with sycamore, then wait for the glue to dry, before turning the whole project down to a smooth, wax burnished finish.

establish the diameter of the former/mould recess, allowing for the different lengths between a hexagon and pentagon.

3 Now, with compass, measure and protractor, make two cardboard templates—a hexagon and a pentagon.

4 Set out your 1 in thick walnut and with a fair degree of accuracy, cut and work the 20 hexagons and the 12 pentagons.

Afterthoughts and modifications

If when you are building up the half-balls, the resin seeps through the joints you will have problems fitting the sycamore wedge strips. So make sure that you seal the joints with the filler paste.

When you are turning down the former, use a convex half-circle template, and aim to cut a perfect hemispherical rece...

The angles between th... pentagons need to be work... settle for a less than perfe... will show when the ball ha...

When you are turning th... ...an ...c a concave half-circle template.

BRICKWORK BOX

John Ambrose

LATHE TYPE
As for the Football Trophy.

TOOLS AND MATERIALS
A full range of tools, as with the Football Trophy, a good selection of face plates, and a number of wooden face plate blanks.

WOODS
You need a quantity of teak, sycamore and box—teak for the various cake-wedge slices, sycamore for the segment veneers, two sycamore blanks for the lid and base mortar rings, and box for the lid boss.

What to do

1 Have a look at the photograph and the working drawings, and see how this project is composed of alternating layers of teak and sycamore. Have a close look at the details and note how there are a greater number of brick rows on the outside of the box than on the inside.

2 When you have studied the details and decided just how big you want your box to be, then set out the wood for the lid and the base, (the teak segments and the sycamore veneers) and build up the two $2\frac{1}{2}$ in thick cake-wedge discs.

3 Run the two thick discs through a saw and part off so that you have two identical 'brick' discs for the base, and two identical 'brick' discs for the lid.

4 This done, take the two blanks/discs of sycamore and mount them onto two small face plates.

5 Working either the lid or the base, take the two identical cake-wedge discs and mount them on two small face plates.

6 Taking note of the diameter of the two cake-wedge discs, cut a recessed wooden blank and mount it on a separate face plate.

7 Take one of the wedge discs, glue its edge,

35

and then mount it in the recessed wooden blank. Note: don't get glue on the face of either the blank or the disc.

8 When the glue is dry, face-up the wood in the recessed blank, and part off the first row of bricks so that its edge is at an accurate 6° to the working face.

9 Leaving the first ring of bricks permanently in the recessed blank, take the 'brick' disc off the lathe.

10 Now mount one of the 'mortar' discs on the lathe, turn its edge off to 6° so that it fits inside the first ring of bricks, then hammer it home and glue it in position.

11 When the glue is dry, part off the sycamore/white wood to leave a $\frac{1}{16}$ in thick ring of mortar.

12 And so continue, working, gluing and wedging alternate 'brick' and 'mortar' discs in the recess mounted master and then parting off,

until you have achieved the desired design. Note: for the best appearance, as the rings get smaller in diameter, so the width of the rings/bricks should be reduced.

13 When you have worked both the base and the lid discs, then clear the workbench and set out the wood for the walls of the box.

14 Take the prepared wood, the eight large segments, the eight small segments and the $\frac{1}{16}$ in thick veneers, and glue them into a cylinder

15 Mount the cylinder between two timber face plates, take it to a good size and finish, mark out the thickness of the first brick ring, and then part off.

16 Now sandwich a disc of thin white 'mortar' wood between the two cylinders, stagger the bricks to achieve a characteristic pattern and then glue and clamp up.

17 And so continue, parting off brick thick-

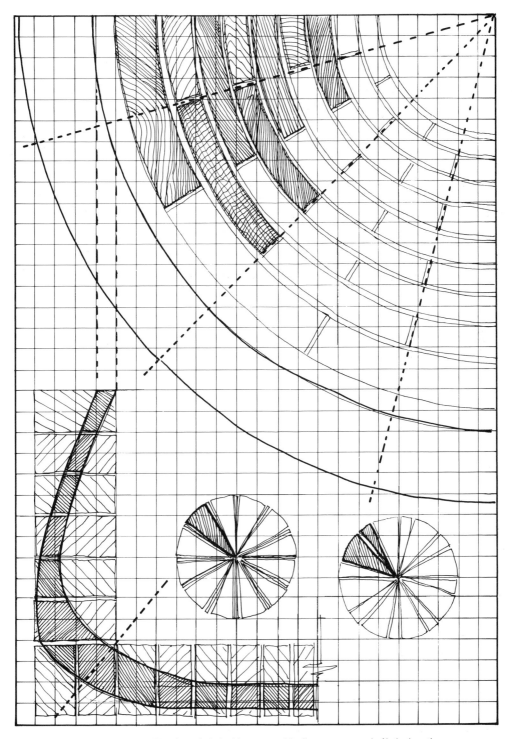

1 Working drawings. Top: the scale is 4 grid squares to 1 in. Bottom: not to scale. Notice how the brick pattern is achieved: the lid has twelve identical wedge slices and twelve veneers, while the base has eight large slices, eight small slices and sixteen veneers. When you come to the final assembly, it is important that the wall-to-base placing is fully considered. In the section the wall is carefully fitted to the base so that the 'mortar' joints are aligned.

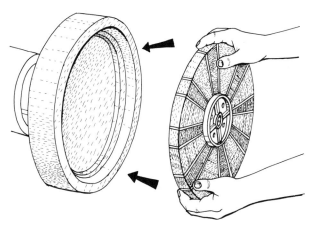

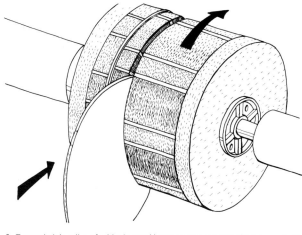

2 When you come to working the base, glue the edge of the wedge-disc and carefully mount it in the recessed wooden blank. Be sure not to put glue on the face of the disc or the face of the blank.

4 To sandwich a disc of white 'mortar' between two courses of bricks, part off and cut through the cylinder, stagger the brick pattern, then glue and clamp up.

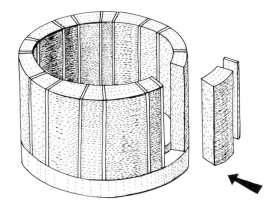

3 When you want to build up the walls of the bowl, take the prepared wood, that is to say the eight large wedges, the eight small wedges and the sixteen veneer slips and glue them together around the face plate mould to make a cylinder.

18 When you have worked both the base and the walls of the box, check with the working drawing for the base/wall placing, then glue the two together so that the brick pattern runs logically, down the walls and across the base.

19 Finally turn off the box profile, cut and work the lid rim, knob and boss and take the wood to a good finish to complete the box.

Afterthoughts and modifications

When you come to turning off the inside curve of the bowl/box, make sure that the profile line runs through the meeting point of the wall/base mortar (see the working drawing section).

When you are turning off successive 6° brick and mortar rings, work them to a good hammer-tight fit. You don't have to wait for the resin glue to cure before going onto the next ring.

nesses, gluing in layers of white 'mortar' wood and so on, until you have achieved a box wall of the desired number of courses.

WINE LADLE

John Ambrose

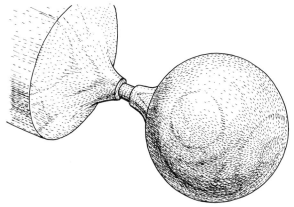

2 Mount your carefully chosen wood on the lathe and turn off a spigotted sphere.

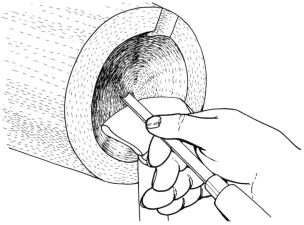

3 Turn off a chuck that has a hemispherical recess. Work the recess to fit the ladle blank, and cut a groove for the spigot.

LATHE TYPE
As with the Football Trophy.

TOOLS AND MATERIALS
A good range of turning tools, as with the Football Trophy project, plus all the usual smaller workshop items.

WOOD
Two pieces of Honduras mahogany.

What to do
1 Have a look at the photographs and the working drawings and notice how the bowl of the ladle has been worked from a sphere, see also how the bowl has been spigoted into the handle.

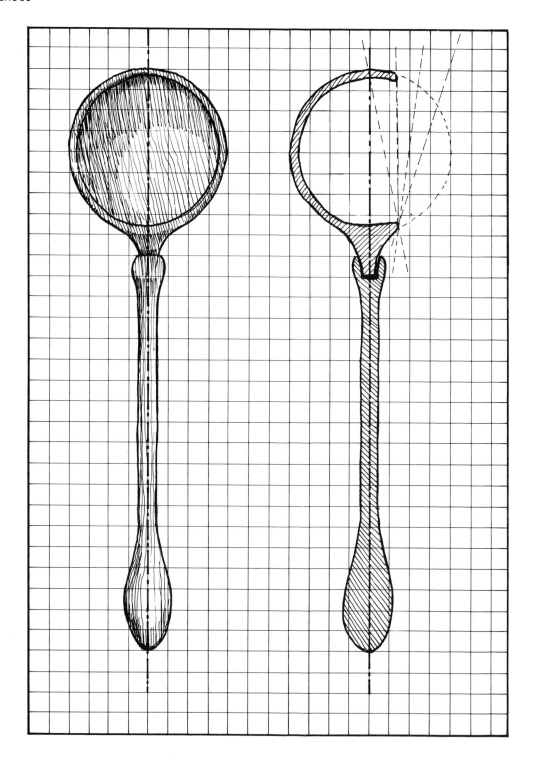

1 Working drawings. The scale is 2 grid squares to 1 in. See how the ladle
bowl is spigotted into the handle and note how the bowl can be hollow turned
to achieve a level or tilted handle-to-rim angle.

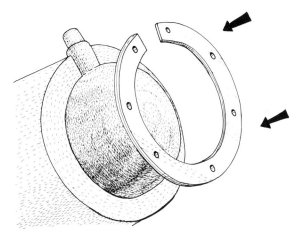

4 Mount the ladle sphere in the recess and then hold it in place with a plywood collar. By easing the spigot up or down through the collar, it is possible to change the bowl-to-handle angle.

2 Noting that you might use a jawed chuck, a special chuck or whatever, mount the wood on the lathe and then with the tools of your choice turn off an exact spigoted sphere.

3 When you have achieved what you consider to be a good spherical smooth-shouldered spigoted form, take the wood to a good finish and part off.

4 Now make a chuck from an 8 × 3 in blank and turn off a smooth well formed hemispherical recess, in other words a recess that fits the ladle.

5 Mount the ladle in the recess and hold it in place with a slotted plywood ring.

6 Adjust the ladle blank so that the handle spigot is at the desired angle and then tighten up the screws so that it is secure.

7 Now hollow turn the ladle bowl to what you consider to be a good thickness and profile, then finish and part off.

8 Turn the handle between centres, take it to a good finish and then glue the bowl spigot into the handle.

Afterthoughts and modifications

When the ladle bowl has been securely contained within the recessed blank, you should just be able to move the handle spigot, the action should be like a ball and socket joint.

If by chance the initial turning is not quite spherical, then the walls of the finished ladle bowl will not be true, use a template to achieve a perfect sphere.

CUP AND SAUCER

John Ambrose

LATHE TYPE
As for the Football Trophy.

TOOLS AND MATERIALS
A good range of turning tools and all the usual workshop tools and materials.

WOODS
For this project you need, a 4 × 4 in blank of burr horse chestnut for the cup, a 5 in diameter blank for the saucer, (thickness to suit) and a small quantity of boxwood for the handle.

1 Working drawings. The scale is approx. 2 grid squares to 1 in. The cup and saucer profile can be worked to suit, notice how the handle is made up from a whole turned ring, and quarter of a turned ring.

What to do

1 Have a look at the project illustrations and the photograph on page 17, see how an interesting burr wood is used for the n•ain forms and a tight close grained wood for the handle. Note how the handle is made up from two turnings—a ring and a ring quarter.

2 Before you put tools to wood, make a series of measured drawings and perhaps modify the forms to suit. You might also at this stage make a set of 'inside' and 'outside' cardboard profile templates.

3 Using the chuck of your choice, (a glue and paper wooden chuck, a collet chuck, a jawed chuck for example), mount the 'cup' blank on the lathe and turn off the simple form.

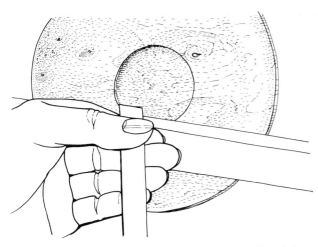

2 Mount the 'saucer' blank on the lathe, turn off a good profile and then establish a recess for the foot of the cup.

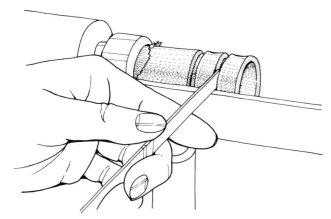

3 When you have turned off a good cylinder, part off two identical hollow-surfaced rings.

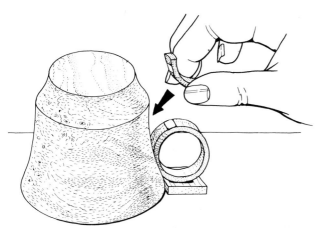

4 Use one whole ring and one quarter ring for the handle, note how the top of the handle is set slightly lower than the cup rim.

4 When you have achieved what you consider to be a good cup profile, take the wood to a smooth finish and part off.

5 Now mount the saucer wood on the lathe, use the callipers to establish the diameter of the foot and cup recess, then take the wood to a good finish and part off.

6 This done, mount the boxwood on the lathe, turn off a blank that is about $1\frac{1}{2}$ ins in diameter and then part off.

7 Now, remount, and hollow turn the blank until you have a cylinder that has an inside diameter of about 1 in.

8 When you have taken the hollow cylinder to a good finish, part off a couple of identical rings.

9 Finally, using a whole ring and quarter of a ring, place, fix and finish the handle, as illustrated.

Afterthoughts and modifications

The success or failure of this project hinges not so much on technical expertize, but rather on the forms being well designed and delicately worked. It is important to spend time at the design stage working up good drawings and making templates.

If you decide to hollow turn the handle with the wood mounted in a jaws chuck, muffle the wood with a protective bandage.

STACKING EGG CUPS

Gerald G. Gilpin

Gerald, a retired architect, formerly a partner in his own practice, first started woodturning in September 1985 when he enrolled for a course at Dartington Technical College. Unhappily, after one of his woodturning lessons, he blacked out in his car suffering what was to be a crippling stroke. Fortunately, Gerald is now on the mend and enjoys lengthy sessions working at his lathe. What he likes most about the craft is its creative aspect, that is to say the exciting and individual characteristics of various woods and the pleasure of handling and using the finished articles. His garage doubles up as a workshop, and although he admits this is rather limiting, it does at the same time promote a tidy and well organized working area. The design process varies, an interesting shape, a spark of an idea, the texture of a particular piece of wood— Gerald finds that a feeling grows as to what he should make next. Finally, before he rejects or accepts an idea, he weighs up all the possibilities by working through a series of sketches and details. The inspiration for this particular project came from a feeling that instead of serving eggs in cups on separate saucers or plates, an all-in-one utensil could be devised that could be stacked and displayed. There is little to add except that Gerald is encouraged by the whole woodturning experience and is now determined to go on to greater things.

LATHE TYPE

Myford ML8 with various attachments, right and left hand face plates, sanding table, three-jaw chuck, grinding wheel, and a combination three-in-one chuck.

TOOLS AND MATERIALS

$\frac{1}{4}$ in spindle gouge
$\frac{1}{2}$ in spindle gouge
scraper
skew chisel
roughing gouge
parting tool
callipers
pencil
measure
workout paper
Garnet paper or graded glass paper
Danish oil
clear polish
various small tools

WOOD

For this project you need a $1\frac{1}{2}$ in thick, 12 in diameter slab of elm for the tray, and a $1\frac{1}{2}$ in thick, 5 in diameter slab of elm for each of the egg cups.

What to do

1 Look at the working drawings and photograph on page 19 and see how the egg cups stack in relation to each other and the tray. Note also how the egg cup section has been designed to take into account the face plate screws.

2 When you have considered all the design and technique implications, mark out your chosen wood, and arrange your tools so that they are close at hand.

3 Mount the 12 in diameter blank on a face plate, check that the wood is secure, then set about turning off the tray. Cut the foot and the

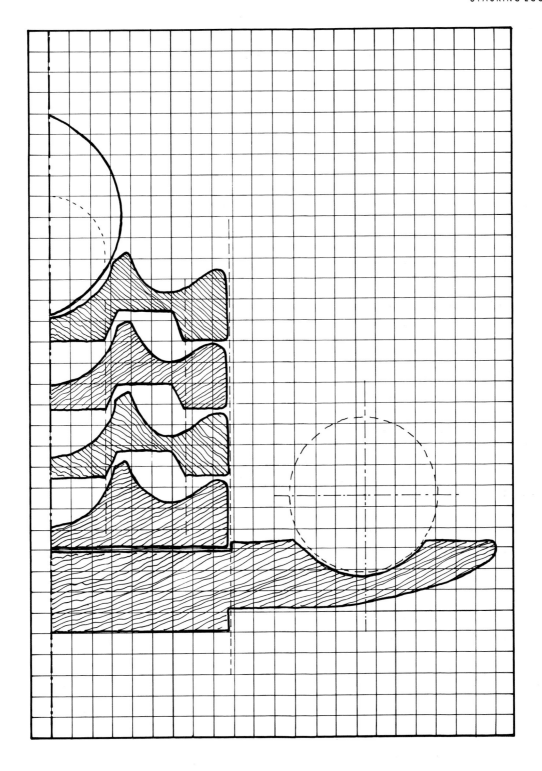

1 Working drawings. The scale is 4 grid squares to 1 in. See how the upper and lower faces of each cup have been designed and worked so that they fit into each other. Note how the face plate screw points have been cut away.

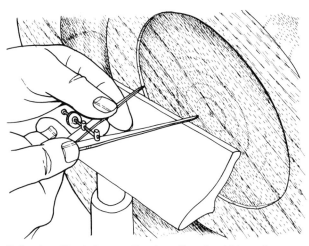

2 Start by making the base tray. Turn the profile and establish a well cut egg cup recess.

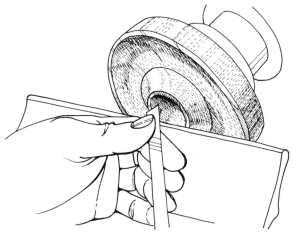

3 When you are turning off the face of the egg cup, it might be as well to refer to a cardboard, template, or a prototype.

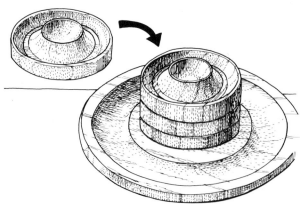

4 The success of this project hinges on the fact that each egg cup is so designed that it stacks on its fellow, so it is most important that each cup is related to a master.

egg cup recess, establish the trough round the tray and generally take the wood to a good finish.

4 When you have cut and worked what you consider to be a good tray profile, take note of the diameter of the cup recess and set out the smaller egg cup blanks accordingly.

5 A piece at a time, mount the 5 in diameter blanks on a face plate, and turn off the upper egg-and-condiment profile. Note the delicate drip splay at the point of contact between the cup and the egg and how the whole upper surface of the cup is nicely contoured.

6 When you have cut and worked the upper face of a set of identical cups, mount a 7 in diameter waster on the lathe and turn off a wooden chuck. Cut the chuck so that the egg cups can be held in a tight secure friction fit.

7 Now, one at a time, mount the egg cups face-in-chuck on the lathe, and take them to a true finish.

8 Take note of the upper cup profile and the position of the face plate screw holes, then cut and work the base trough.

9 Finally, when the tray and all the cups come together to make a well considered stack, take the whole project to a good finish, lay on three well brushed coats of Danish oil, then burnish the wood with a clear polish using a clean brush.

Afterthoughts and modifications

Gerald uses a face plate and a home made wooden chuck but you might re-design the project slightly and use an expanding collet chuck.

Have a look at the working drawings and see how there are four egg cups in all, three with base troughs and one without. You might work it so that all the cups have a trough, then they can be stacked at random.

ACORN SEWING TIDY

Colin Hovland

Armed with only Frank Pain's book, *The Practical Woodturner*, Colin Hovland decided that he would like to take up the craft. Without the benefit of personal instruction his progress was, at first, somewhat frustrated by the inevitable mistakes of a beginner but he persevered and slowly and surely he acquired the skills of the craft. All that was about ten years ago and now, as this project must surely show, Colin is a confident and able woodturner. So confident, in fact, that he is prepared to share his woodturning experiences by giving demonstrations at craft shows. He very much enjoys passing on advice to keen beginners—particularly those who are eager to gain information and ideas.

Inspired by the numerous questions he is asked at various craft shows, he has now started to compile a series of articles and designs with a view of publishing a book on woodturning projects in the near future.

Working in his 12 × 10 ft garden workshop he is surrounded by the equipment that he has collected over the years—his lathe, a bandsaw, a circular saw, a planer, a pillar drill and all the rest. Colin is able to take his time and turns work to an extremely high standard. As for project ideas, he usually draws them from his own observations and from the published work of other turners. However, there is nothing Colin likes better than the challenge of being commissioned or requested to make something out of the ordinary.

LATHE TYPE
Coronet Major with a 1 HP motor.

TOOLS AND MATERIALS
$\frac{3}{4}$ in roughing gouge
round nosed scraper
small square ended scraper
$\frac{1}{8}$ to $\frac{1}{4}$ in parting tool
$\frac{1}{2}$ in skew chisel
$\frac{1}{4}$ in spindle gouge
$\frac{1}{2}$ in drill bit
$\frac{7}{8}$ in bit
callipers
workout paper
measure
cellulose sealer
wax and of course all the usual workshop tools and materials

WOOD
A $6\frac{1}{2}$ in long blank of Kingwood.

What to do

1 Look at the working drawings and photograph on page 15, and see how the three little turnings come together to make a very nicely designed double-lidded, acorn-shaped container.

2 When you have considered the various ways that this project might be worked and have modified it to suit your chuck specifications then mount your wood on the lathe and turn off a $1\frac{5}{8}$ in diameter cylinder.

3 Now, with the wood turning between centres, in a collet chuck or whatever and working with the tools of your choice, turn off the outside profiles of the three units, the base, the thimble and the lid.

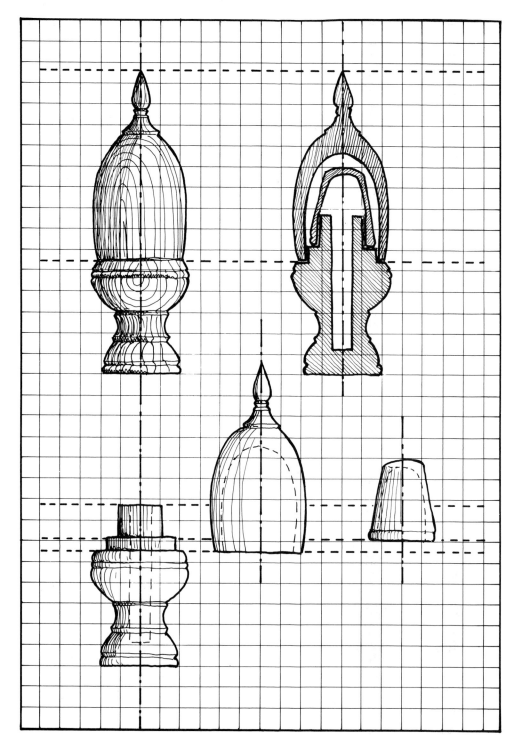

1 Working drawings. The scale is 4 grid squares to 1 in. See how the three little turnings all come together to make the acorn-shaped form, and note how the two lids, that is to say the outer lid and the inner thimble lid, both sit on the stepped and drilled base.

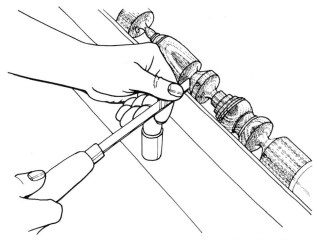

2 Secure the wood between centres and work the three turnings. Use callipers to achieve the various profiles and steps.

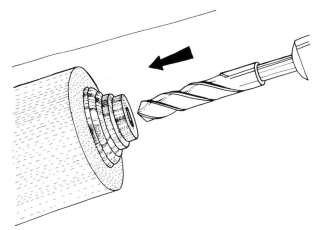

3 Secure the base in a wooden chuck, and then use a $\frac{1}{4}$ in drill bit to work a $1\frac{5}{8}$ in deep hole. Note: you can mount the wood in a special chuck, a jawed chuck or whatever.

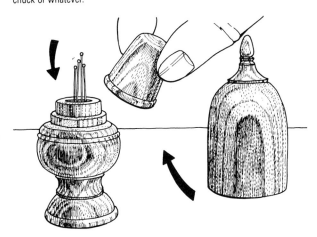

4 When you are finishing off (rubbing down, polishing, waxing), stop from time to time and make sure that you haven't altered the fit.

4 When you have taken all three turnings to a good size and finish, gently part off.

5 Bearing in mind that you might change the order of working or the techniques to suit, support the sewing tidy base in a wooden chuck and then use a $\frac{1}{4}$ in drill to work a hole that is about $1\frac{5}{8}$ ins deep.

6 When you have established the depth and diameter of the hole for the needles, work the square-cut lid and thimble steps using callipers and your chosen tools.

7 Take note of the diameter and depth of the stepped base, then mount the thimble in a wooden chuck and remove the bulk of its interior waste with a $\frac{1}{2}$ in diameter drill.

8 Turn and turn about, work both the base and the thimble, until the thimble is a good fit.

9 Mount the lid in a wooden chuck, clear away the bulk of the waste with a $\frac{7}{8}$ in diameter bit, and then use the round nosed scraper to take the wood to a good finish.

10 Finally, check that after sealing and waxing the three turnings come together for a good fit, and the job is done.

Afterthoughts and modifications

This project could be worked using, a pin chuck, a spigot chuck, a split ring chuck, a cup chuck, a collect chuck, the tapered hole in the headstock spindle, and so on.

If you do decide to use a wooden chuck with a tapered hole and the tailpiece, make sure, at the parting off stage, that you only use very light pressure with the tailpiece.

When you are working the inside of the thimble and the lid, withdraw the tailstock so that it's well away from the work and re-set the tool rest at the end of the workpiece.

The method described here is not precisely that which Colin Hoveland used, as he made various adaptions for his own lathe, tools and technique. Shape the project to suit your own lathe and chuck specifications.

SKEWED BOWL

Ian Walton

A research scientist by profession, Ian first started woodturning in 1983, when he inherited a rather basic drill-powered lathe from his uncle. Since that date, he has graduated to a Coronet Hobby lathe with several attachments. He particularly appreciates woodturning because he has always been creative and it gives him the opportunity to make decorative and functional items to his own designs. He also derives a great deal of pleasure from making turned items as presents, in the knowledge that the personal touch is appreciated by the recipient. In addition, the craft provides for Ian a form of relaxation which is a totally absorbing contrast to his work as a research scientist.

The inspiration for specific designs usually springs from experimental workouts with off-cuts and if a piece 'turns out' well, he upgrades the project, and works with selected wood. He usually makes and follows detailed and accurate drawings, but if the finished prototype doesn't look right, then the project is invariably scrapped. However, once a successful prototype has been achieved it is taken through a modification programme, in other words the project is adjusted until the best features of the wood are realized. Ian finds that working in this way not only assists the general design process but it also helps him to learn more about the craft. Ian admits that learning by doing, or learning by making mistakes, is a slow method but at the same time, it is perhaps the best way to absorb the necessary skills.

What inspired him to make the skewed bowl? He specifically wanted to make a break with the rather hackneyed English tradition of turning symmetrical forms. The resulting bowl success-fully answers the brief in that it does not possess any of the usual symmetrical turned object characteristics, and yet it has been entirely hand turned.

LATHE TYPE
Two year old Coronet Hobby lathe with a $\frac{1}{2}$ HP motor and a selection of face plates.

TOOLS AND MATERIALS
$\frac{3}{8}$ in long and strong bowl gouge
$\frac{1}{2}$ in scraper
wedge shaped wooden face plate (angle to suit)
metal face plate
callipers
pencil
measure
workout paper
sanding sealer
friction polish
wax
and the usual workshop tools and items

WOOD
Blank of ash of a size to suit.

What to do

1 Study the working drawings and the photograph on page 22 and see how the blank has been distanced from the face plate by a wedge. Notice that but for the wedge, the project is a very basic bowl turned form.

2 When you understand just how the project is to be achieved, mount the ash blank on a wooden wedge-shaped face plate (you can use paper and glue, screws or whatever), and then

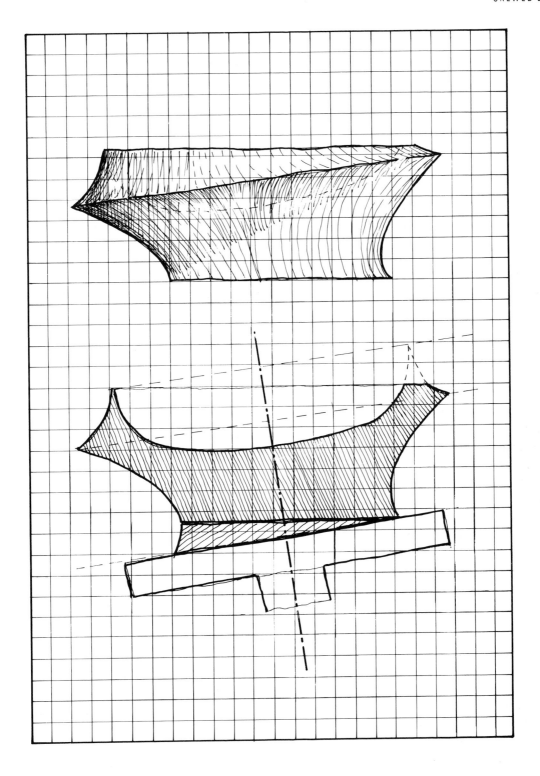

1 Working drawings. The scale is approx. 3 grid squares to 1 in. Note in the section how, but for the face plate wedge, the project is bowl-turned in the traditional manner.

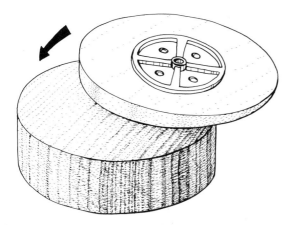

2 Once you have selected a choice piece of wood, mount both the wood and the wedge on a face plate.

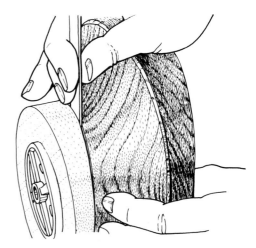

4 Finally, remove both the wedge and the face plate, and make good the base and the rim.

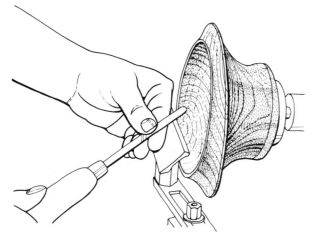

3 When turning the inside of the bowl, take care that the skewed face doesn't snatch at your tools, work with extra care and caution.

5 Aim to work the whole form so that all the edges and angles are crisp and clean cut, then, with sanding sealer, friction polish and wax, take the wood to a good finish.

6 Finally, with great care, take the bowl off the lathe, remove the wedge and face plate and make good.

Afterthoughts and modifications

When you are choosing your wood, select timber that is flawless, reject material that appears to have dead knots, a twisted loose grain, or any splits.

If, at the start of the project, you are in doubt as to how the wedged blank will look once it has been turned, make a prototype. Try working the project using several different wedge sections. You might modify this project by having two wedges; the profile could be partially worked, one wedge could be removed and then the form could be taken to completion.

When you come to working the delicate rim, stop for a moment and take your tools to a keen edge.

mount both the blank and the wedges securely on a metal face plate. Note: you can of course use a chuck special rather than a metal face plate.

3 Check that the wood is secure and then with the tools of your choice, turn off the outside bowl profile, watch out for wood judder.

4 When you have achieved what you consider to be a good form, hollow turn the inside of the bowl, bearing in mind that the wedge mounted blank will snatch at the tools.

CHRISTMAS TABLE CENTRE

Trevor Christopher Andrews

Trevor, a telephone engineer by profession, has always enjoyed woodturning, he finds it a relaxing and inspirational hobby. His interest first started at school, but unfortunately, like many people, when he left school, he left behind all his woodturning opportunities. Many years later, however, he decided to buy a lathe. He started with a small basic model, and then went on to invest in an ELU DB180, a sophisticated machine with a great deal of potential.

Now he has turned his car out into the cold, and transformed his garage into a workshop. Into this relatively modest area he has set up all his equipment, his lathe, a bandsaw he made himself, all his small tools, and of course his stock of wood.

What Trevor enjoys most about the craft, is the ability to turn a piece of rough timber into an item of pleasure. To see the grain emerging from the wood as it is being turned, to see the changing colours, to be able to create all manner of uniquely beautiful shapes, designs and forms and to be able to build a single item from a great many individual turned units—for Trevor these are the real pleasures of woodturning.

LATHE TYPE
An ELU DB180 $1\frac{1}{2}$ HP lathe with a selection of chucks.

TOOLS AND MATERIALS
Sorby $\frac{1}{4}$ in roughing out gouge
$\frac{1}{4}$ in parting tool
1 in skew chisel
$\frac{1}{4}$ in gouge
$\frac{1}{2}$ in gouge
$1\frac{1}{4}$ in saw tooth bit

$\frac{1}{2}$ in beading chisel
coping saw
compass
workout paper
cellulose sanding sealer
wire wool
carnauba and beeswax (melted down in genuine turpentine)
and all the usual more general tools and materials

WOODS
For this project you need Iroko off-cuts for the candle holders, the paddle joining pieces, and

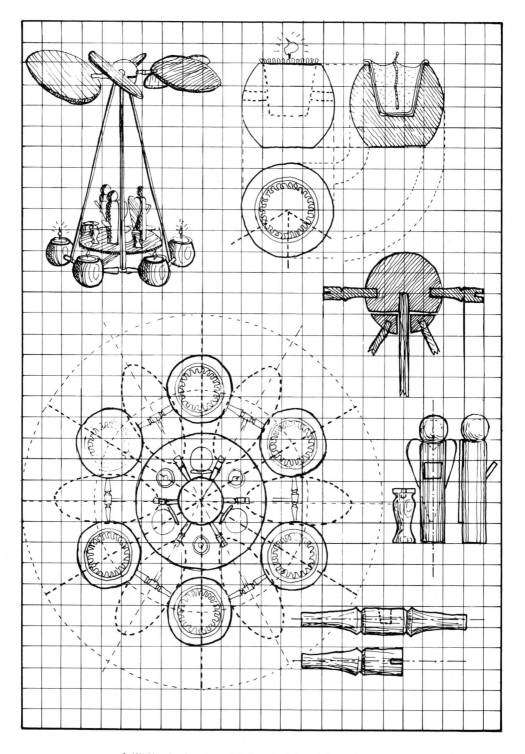

1 Working drawings. Lower left: the scale of the main layout is approx. 1 grid square to 1 inch. All the other details and sections are not to scale. See how the overall design theme is based on a hexagonal layout and note also how the various details relate to very basic forms.

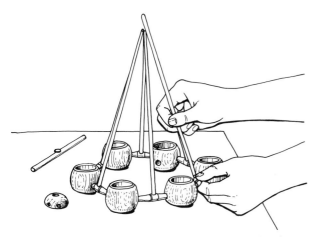

2 When you have turned off the six bowls and the various spindles, then you can start putting the project together. Have a dry run fitting before you use glue.

4 Finally, when the main structure has been put together, trim the angles and check that all is correct. Note: it is most important that all the components are finely fitted and balanced.

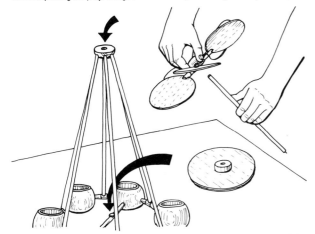

3 Once you have cut, glued and placed the bowls, the spindles, the six upright dowels and the top bearing, then you can fit the paddle and the drive shaft. See how there is a nail-point bearing at the end of the shaft, and a nail-head bearing on the lower cross-beam.

the various spindles and the angels, a quantity of Burbinga veneer off-cuts for the paddles, the angel wings, and the details. You also need a quantity of shop-bought dowel for the various structural rods. Note: Trevor obtained the Burbinga from a boat builder.

What to do

1 First of all have a close look at the photographs and the working drawing details, and see how the rather complex, hot air mobile has been put together. Note how the hot air paddles are fixed to the top half of a ball, and how the

central paddle-shaft passes through the bottom half of the ball to be pivoted on a nail–head bearing.

2 With a pencil, measure, workout paper and a compass, draw up your designs to size, and then trace and transfer the lines to your various pieces of wood.

3 Take your coping saw and cut out the various discs, the main turn-table and the six paddle discs. With a piece of scrap timber larger than the circle required and another piece the same size as that of the finished article, sandwich the veneer square between these two pieces. With tailstock pressure the veneer will stay in place and with a sharp chisel the circle can be cut out. Six can be cut out the same size for the paddles and two for the base for strength. Rub the discs down to a smooth finish with graded glasspaper.

4 Take the six blocks of Iroko, check them over for possible problems, then, block by block, screw them to a small face plate or screw chuck and set about turning off the six identical candle pots. Open the pots out so that they are large enough to take crinkle edge foil-cup night lights. Take the wood to a good finish.

5 Now, working between centres, or using a

special chuck, set about turning off all the little spindles, that is the six $2\frac{1}{2}$ in long pot-linking bails, and the six paddle holders.

6 Take the two pieces of Iroko that make up the central split ball and then working them a piece at a time, turn off the two domes that go to make up the ball-like form at the top of the mobile.

7 Note the size and design of the three little angel 'skittles', then working between centres or with a special chuck, turn off the simple head-and-body forms.

8 Set out and cut the three pieces of Burbinga that make up the heart shaped angel wings. Rub the wood down to a good smooth finish.

9 When you have cut and worked all the various pieces for the project, clear the worksurface of all clutter and dust, and then set out your working drawings, the hand drill, all the small tools, and the glue.

10 Mark out and drill the six candle holders, note the 120° angle of the holes, and also how two of the cups are drilled to take the main pivotal strut.

11 Drill the six cup-linking bails and the paddle ball. (All the drilling for this project can be done with the workpieces still on the lathe using a dividing head and electric drill.)

12 Now with great care, start to put the project together. Link the six cups, and then arrange the six 12 in long dowels so that they spring up from the bails.

13 Set the main pivotal strut out with a nail-head bearing, and then place it in position.

14 Gather the ends of the six 12 in long dowels, and locate them in the six holes on the underside of the central ball.

15 Cut and work the six paddle holders, set them in the top half of the central paddle ball, then set the paddle discs in the holders and arrange them at a suitable angle.

16 Now fix and arrange the central table-turning rod so that it passes through the top bearing, and through the turn-table. Tip the dowel with a hardened nail, and then rest it on the nail-head pivot point.

17 Finally, set out, trim and arrange the various decorative details, then bring all the wood to a polished finish.

Afterthoughts and modifications

The whole project is based on a hexagonal theme. This being so, at the design stage, all points can be struck off with a compass.

The nail-head bearing is rather primitive. You might re-design this feature, and use, say, a hung turn-table and a cup-supported central pivotal rod.

The angle at which the hot air paddles are fixed is critical, the angle is best decided by trial and error.

CAUTION

Obviously great care must be taken when using this Christmas Table Centre to ensure that the flames do not come anywhere near the paddles or struts of the wood or that it is left unattended.

COOPERED JEWEL BOX

Arthur Anslow

Arthur has always been interested in woodwork, making everything from furniture to clock cases. He first became hooked on woodturning after reading an article in *Practical Woodworking* magazine by the late Geoff Peters. Once bitten by the bug, Arthur went out and bought himself a Coronet Major CMB 600 $\frac{3}{4}$ HP 5-speed lathe, a lathe with a $4\frac{1}{2}$ in and 23 in swing and 33 ins between centres. His double garage workshop is well kitted out with a workbench, a free standing band saw, an 8 in bench saw, a double grinder, a drill stand and a treadle fretsaw bought in 1939. Also, as you might expect from a man who has spent most of his life working with farm machinery, he has hand tools almost beyond count.

As to Arthur's working methods, he first of all lets his mind play around with an idea, then he makes rough sketches and talks it over with his wife who acts as his design consultant. If she gives him the go-ahead, then he gets down to work and draws out plans and maybe even makes a dummy run using off-cuts. Finally, if an idea seems to be working out, Arthur selects the perfect piece of wood for the project and starts the actual turning.

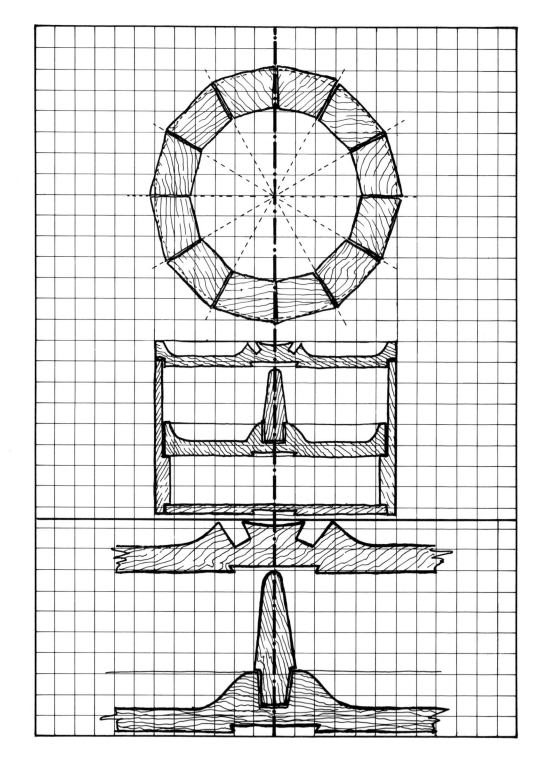

1 Working drawings. Top: The scale is approx. 2 grid squares to 1 in. Bottom: the scale is 4 grid squares to 1 in. See how the initial block is made up from twelve coopered staves, note angles and the relative placing of the tiers.

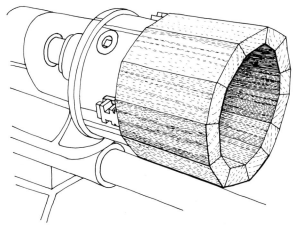

2 Mount the coopered tube on the lathe, and very carefully turn it down to a 6 in outside diameter.

4 The tiers need to be a good smooth slide fit, allow some slight leeway to accommodate wood movement.

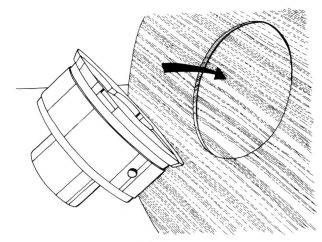

3 When you come to turning the various discs that make up the tiers, work a recessed undercut and secure to the lathe with a 1 in expanding chuck.

LATHE TYPE
Coronet Major CMB 600, with a $\frac{3}{4}$ HP motor, 5 speeds, a $4\frac{1}{2}$ in swing and 33 ins between centres. You will need a face plate and three chucks—a 3 jaw scroll, a screw and a 1 in expanding.

TOOLS AND MATERIALS
bench saw or similar for cutting the staves
1 in roughing gouge
power plane
1 in skew chisel
$\frac{1}{4}$ in skew chisel
$\frac{3}{8}$ in gouge
wire wool
Craft Lac
wax
You will also need:
glue
pencils
paper
measure
callipers
template card
scissors
and all the usual workshop tools

WOOD
A quantity of American Black Walnut—amount to suit the project or your modifications.

What to do

THE MAIN BODY
1 Look at the working drawings and see how the coopered box is made up from 12 angle-edged staves, then cut and plane your wood to size.

2 Glue, place and clamp the staves, and leave them to cure for at least 72 hours.

3 Secure the stave built tube on the three jaw scroll chuck, and turn down to a 6 in outside diameter.

4 Making sure that you keep the sides parallel, turn down the inside of the tube.

THE CENTRAL TIER AND THE RING TREE

5 Using the $\frac{1}{4}$ in skew chisel, and reversing the wood on the chuck if necessary, cut and work the various inside diameters, the step for the central tier and the step for the base.

6 The main cylinder cut, mount a blank on the screw chuck, and work a disc for the central tier.

7 Turn down the base of the central disc and cut a recess for the 1 in expanding chuck.

8 Turn down the disc edge until it is a good sliding fit in the main body, then bore a $\frac{1}{2}$ in blind $\frac{1}{2}$ hole in its centre.

9 Now turn the various profiles as shown on the working drawings, or shape to suit.

10 Finally turn down a stem for the ring tree, cut a stepped spigot and then glue cure, turn and finish.

THE TOP TIER OR LID

11 Using short screws located in an area that is to be wasted, mount a blank on the face plate.

12 Turn the base of the lid to the dimensions shown, and cut a recess for the expanding chuck.

13 Mount the lid on the expanding chuck, and turn the integral handle/knob and contours to suit.

14 Finally take to a good fit and finish.

BASE OF BOX AND FINISHING

15 Turn a disc with a recess for the expanding chuck.

16 Glue the base disc into the main body recess, turn to a good finish, and then work the base so that it is slightly concave. Mount the box and lid together on the lathe to ensure a perfect match.

17 Finally, seal, work the whole box with wire wool, brush on a coat of Craft Lac, or similar, and bring to a good finish with wax.

Afterthoughts and modifications

If you don't want to use off-cuts, then the main body of the box can be cut from solid wood.

You can use a single, special multi chuck rather that the chucks described.

The integral recessed lid/knob is a tricky feature, it might be as well to experiment with scrap wood.

The bottom of the inner box and the central tier can be covered with green baize.

Leaving out the recess and centre tier and adding a suitable lining makes an excellent biscuit barrel.

HUMPTY TOY

Kenneth Biggs

In 1949 Ken won the school prize for wood-work, an achievement that set the pace for all that was to follow. His working experiences are many and varied, an apprenticeship in marine engineering, national service in the navy, designing in a drawing office and then redundancy. Ken is now working at the Open University. He has a great many hobbies and interests, from playing in a dance band to dingy sailing and photography. In the past he also built model steam engines and numerous other things. It is fair to say that Ken is a keen all-round craftsman. This being so, when he decided to take up woodturning, he didn't pop out to the nearest woodturning stockist, but, characteristically, he started building his own lathe. The designs were drawn out, materials gathered, and then before his family could say a word, Ken had made a very nice $\frac{1}{4}$ HP machine.

With his first project, a spinning wheel, working drawings were obtained, studied and corrected and museum examples were researched. Then, as with all the other projects that were to follow, Ken worked with enthusiasm and gusto. He enjoys the challenge of woodturning, he likes to work with exotic timbers and perhaps most important of all, he likes to give a project, everything he has. As to what inspired this particular piece of work, Ken was playing in the bath with a piece of soap, and then . . . Eurika! . . . the Humpty idea was born!

LATHE TYPE
A home made $\frac{1}{4}$ HP lathe with a 18 in turning diameter and a 24 in long bed.

TOOLS AND MATERIALS
selection of woodturning gouges
parting tool
hand drill and selection of drill bits
drum sander or hand-held glasspaper
callipers
pencil
measure
workout paper
sanding sealer
Briwax
wood glue
junior hacksaw
coping saw or the use of a bandsaw
short length of $\frac{1}{8}$ in diameter brass/steel for the pins
3 in long piece of $\frac{3}{8} \times \frac{1}{8}$ in mildsteel for the lever
small hinge
various small screws
couple of pieces of coloured felt
all the usual smaller tools

WOODS
A piece of hardwood $3 \times 3 \times 6$ ins for the head, various pieces of $1 \times 1\frac{3}{4} \times \frac{5}{8}$ in off-cuts for the bricks, strips of $\frac{1}{8}$ in thick softwood for the mortar and off-cuts of hardwood for the base.

What to do
1 Look at the working drawings and the photograph on page 20, and see how the Humpty is operated by a simple see-saw lever and a length of $\frac{1}{8}$ in diameter rod. Note also how the lower half of the head is hinged.

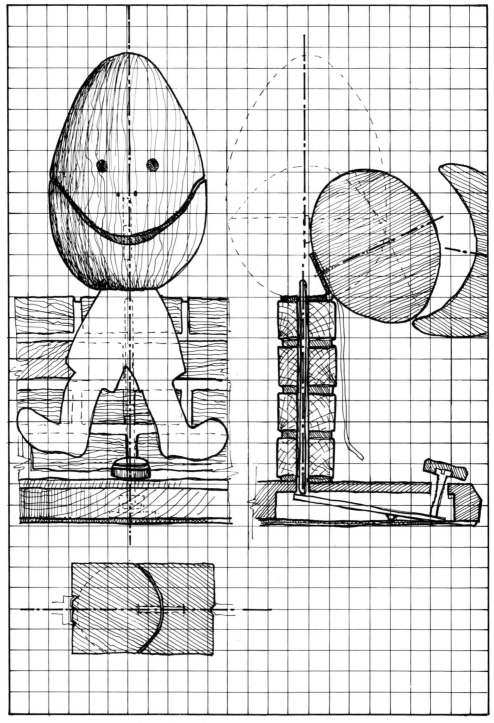

1 Working drawings. The scale is 4 grid squares to 1 in. This project is slightly tricky in that it is necessary to make the little metal screw-and-rod see-saw mechanism. Note how, when the thumb button is pressed down, a rod is pushed up so as to tilt Humpty off his wall, and see also, how the 'egg' block is sawn and pinned before being turned between centres.

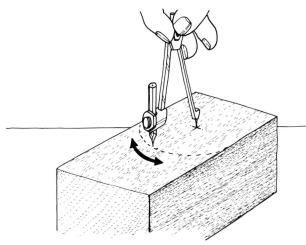

2 Take the prepared 'egg' wood, set the compass to a radius of 1½ ins, then strike off the line of the mouth.

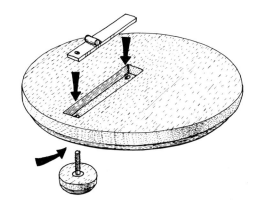

3 When you have trenched a recess at the back of the base plate, drill the 'pin' and 'button' holes, and then have a dry run fitting, just to make sure that the mechanism works.

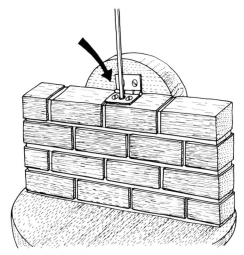

4 Build up the wall with wooden 'bricks', glue and strip wood 'mortar', then fit, hinge, and locate Humpty so that the ⅛ in diameter rod tilts him off his perch.

2 When you have studied the project and worked out all the details, mark out your wood and arrange all your tools and materials so that they are easily to hand.

3 Take the piece of $3 \times 3 \times 6$ in of hardwood, set out the line of the mouth with a compass fixed at a radius of $1\frac{1}{2}$ ins and strike off an arc (see the working drawings).

4 Once you have established the position of the mouth, take a coping or bandsaw and cut through the 3×3 in block.

5 Once the line of the mouth has been worked, centre and drill the two halves of the wood and then fit them back together with a $\frac{1}{8}$ in diameter pin (see the working drawing for the detail).

6 Now secure the 6 in length of hardwood between centres, and then, with the tools of your choice, turn off a classic egg form.

7 Take the egg to a good finish, drill out the eyes and the nostrils and remove the pin.

8 Mark out and prepare the $6 \times 6 \times \frac{5}{8}$ in piece of hardwood, mount it on a face plate and then turn off a well finished base disc.

9 With a router (or the tool of your choice), cut a trench recess at the back of the base and fit the see-saw lever.

10 Once you have positioned the lever, marked out the $\frac{1}{8}$ in diameter pin hole, and generally checked that all is well, set about building the little wall.

11 Once the wall is about 3 ins high, finish off and make good. When the glue is dry, drill a $\frac{5}{32}$ in diameter hole down through the wall and into the base cavity.

12 Now work the egg so that it sits on the wall, then cut, fit and fix, the felt trousers-and-feet profile and the brass hinge.

13 When the egg is well placed and fitted, drill through the brass hinge and fit the $\frac{1}{8}$ in diameter rod.

14 Adjust the see-saw lever and the rod, then cut and fix the $\frac{1}{16}$ in thick ply base.

15 Finally, when the Humpty can be tilted and tipped at the press of the button, take the wood to a good finish and burnish with wax.

Afterthoughts and modifications

This project is tricky only because of the little bit of metalwork, you might modify the project and have perhaps a wooden sea-saw and a dowel rod.

Ken cut out a slot for the lever mechanism, you might work a recess on the lathe.

Although Ken has left the wood unstained, you might prefer to have the whole project worked in bright primary colours. If this is the case, use either model makers' gloss enamels, or quick-drying acrylics and a varnish. Note: the paints must be non-toxic.

COIN HOLDER

William Norman Clarke

Norman dabbled with woodturning at school and also at home on an old wooden framed lathe, he only took to the craft seriously seven or eight years ago. Since that date however, he has read up on the subject and has attended a very helpful two day course. A one-time agricultural engineer with a farming background, he is now a farm manager living in a large old farmhouse. His outhouse workshop is about 17 × 10 ft and into this very useful space he has put two lathes, an Emco and a Tyme Avon, a sawbench, a small bandsaw, and of course all the usual hand tools. For Norman, woodturning is an art form; he is always striving for the ideal, for the perfect balance between function, design, technique and texture. When it comes to designing however, he rarely draws out a project, but rather prefers to sketch out a few ideas on scraps of paper and then work towards the finished piece as in his minds eye. Norman has ample supplies of local wood—elm, apple, yew, hawthorn to name a few and he has in the past used everything from beech to bog oak. He usually makes his coin holders out of carefully selected and seasoned fruit wood. Inspiration to make this particular project came from his wife's metal coin holder. He appreciated it would be difficult to make one in wood and realized that he might need to modify his tools, but then Norman enjoys a challenge.

LATHE TYPE
Tyme Avon with a $\frac{3}{4}$ HP motor and a Craft Supplies precision chuck.

TOOLS AND MATERIALS
roughing gouge
$\frac{1}{4}$ in spindle gouge
$\frac{1}{2}$ in skew chisel
$\frac{5}{8}$ in or a $\frac{9}{16}$ in twist drill
couple of hook-shaped scrapers, Norman made his own
pencil
measure
callipers
workout paper
glasspaper
with Melamine finish or a friction polish
spring to suit
all the usual workshop tools and materials

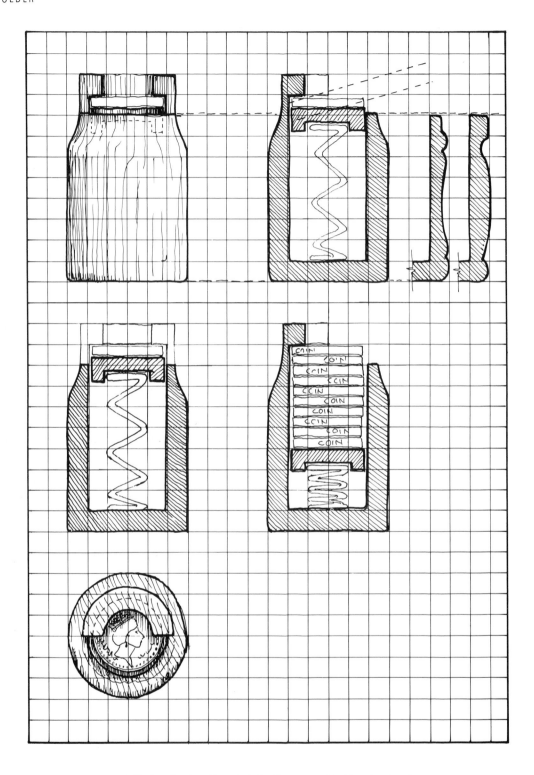

1 Working drawings. The scale is 4 grid squares to 1 in. Note the relatively simple construction and how the coin push is recessed and located under the container's half-rim. Note also the angle of entry for the coin push.

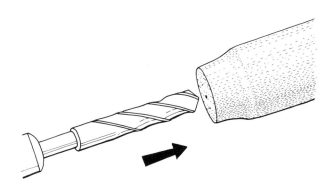

2 Bore out the centre of the blank to a depth of about $2\frac{1}{4}$ in.

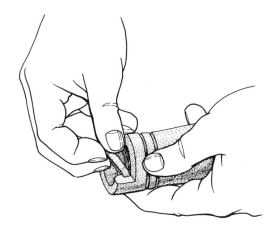

4 When you have worked the two turnings, pop the spring into the holder, angle the coin push and then slide it under the slotted half-rim.

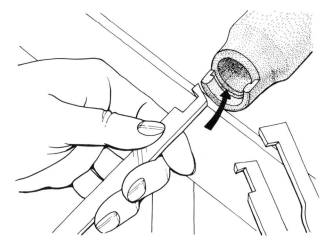

3 When you have cut away the half-rim, take one or other of the specially ground hooked scrapers, and turn out the inside rim slot. Note: stop the lathe before withdrawing the scraper.

WOOD

$2 \times 2 \times 6$ in fruit wood off-cut, apple, pear or cherry, just about any dense grained dry timber can be used.

What To Do

1 First have a look at the working drawings and details, and see how, although the inside of the holder needs to be worked to a set size, the outside can be turned to just about any design that takes your fancy.

2 Take your chosen wood, and check it for quality, reject any wood that looks less than perfect.

3 Using a chuck, one with split rings, jaws or whatever, mount the wood on the lathe, and turn off the basic cylindrical profile.

4 When you have achieved what you consider to be a good initial form, take the $\frac{5}{8}$ in diameter or the $\frac{9}{16}$ in diameter twist drill, and bore out the $2\frac{1}{2}$ in long cylinder to a depth of about $2\frac{1}{4}$ ins.

5 Now, with the tools of your choice, enter the $\frac{5}{8}$ in diameter bore hole, establish the $\frac{3}{4}$ in depth of the rim/coin stop, then work the inside mouth/rim of the cylinder, until it's about $\frac{11}{16}$ in in diameter, (see the working drawings).

6 When you have established the clean, square-cut face of the stepped rim (the coin/plunger stop), then round off the outside rim and mark off all round with a pencil about $\frac{1}{2}$ in from the end. The outside rim should now measure about $1\frac{1}{4}$ ins in diameter.

7 Now, complete with the chuck, remove the wood from the lathe, and saw straight down to the pencil mark to establish the half-circle rim collar.

8 Return the wood to the lathe, cut away the half-rim, and then use a special hooked scraper to hollow turn the inside–rim coin slot.

9 Open up the barrel to a depth of about $2\frac{1}{4}$ ins, aim to taper up from a 1 in diameter bottom, to a $\frac{7}{8}$ in diameter rim.

10 Now turn down the outside profile to a good design, fit, finish and then part off.

11 Refer to the working drawings, then use a scrap of waste to turn off the little $\frac{7}{8}$ in diameter recessed coin push/plunger. With care there should be enough wood left from the holder to make the plunger from and so ensure a matching finish.

12 When you have worked the two turnings to a good size and finish, clear the bench of all clutter and set out the spring, polishes and other bits and pieces required.

13 Finally, pop the spring into the holder, enter the plunger/coin push into the mouth of the holder at an angle of about 45° engage it under the rim, and the job is done.

Afterthoughts and modifications

You might of course modify this project to take just about any coin of your choice.

The depth of the coin plunger, and the amount of rim that you cut away, these are both critical features, if in doubt make a prototype.

When you are choosing your spring, choose one that has nicely balanced push and compression characteristics, a loose coiled spring about $\frac{5}{8}$ in diameter and $2\frac{1}{2}$ ins long will do just fine.

If the timber is damp, you will have ovality problems, choose your wood with care.

RACK OF COAT PEGS

Dick Crowther

Dick was an officer with the Forestry Commission for all his professional life, and so has been involved with and interested in wood for a long time. Naturally enough, when he retired his hobbies tended to focus on woodwork. His interest in woodturning was stimulated by the need for a set of large drawer knobs for a tallboy. Working on his son's model makers' lathe and inspired by his first efforts, his interest soon grew, until it culminated in attending evening classes in woodturning.

Dick followed up this venture by purchasing an Arundel lathe. This, together with an old 7 in circular saw, a band saw and a work bench, all set up in half of a double garage, now form the hub of his woodturning activities. The rack project was sparked off when he wanted to replace some wire coat pegs in the ringing chamber of his parish church. It hasn't stopped there—Dick is now planning to sell his turnings at local craft fairs. As for suitable wood, he has used everything from robinia and small round-wood obtained from a firewood merchant, to pieces given to him by friends.

LATHE TYPE
Arundel M230 $\frac{3}{4}$ HP lathe with a screw chuck, a del, a face plate and a wooden chuck.

TOOLS AND MATERIALS
roughing gouge
spindle gouge
parting tool
1 in Forstner bit

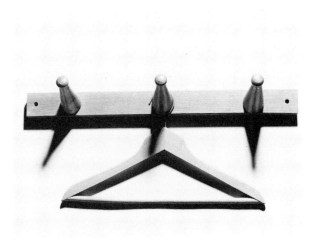

wooden chuck on a faceplate
Bri Wax
pencils
callipers
workout paper
and all the usual workshop tools

WOOD
For each peg you need a piece of wood about $6 \times 2\frac{1}{2} \times 2\frac{1}{2}$ ins, the base plate can be of a size to suit.

What to do

1 First have a good long look at the working drawings and see how the pegs have been turned, off-set and then re-turned. See how the pegs have been flanged and angled so that coats do not slip off.

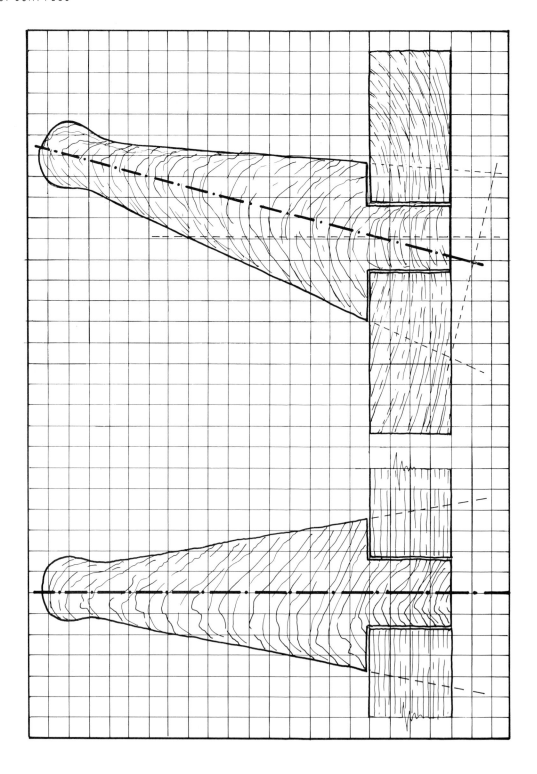

1 Working drawings. The scale is 4 grid squares to 1 in. See how the peg has been turned as a straightforward cone and how the spigot has been worked by turning the cone off-centre.

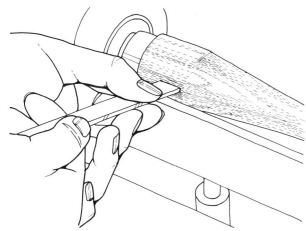

2 Check your wood over for possible problems, then turn the pegs between centres. Allow for the slight swelling at the end of the peg, the base flange or shoulder, and the spigot. Take the wood to a good finish.

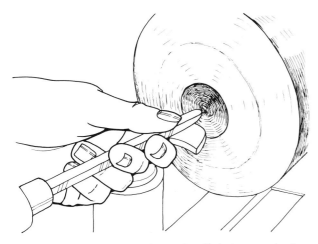

3 Turn off a wooden chuck and work a peg-shaped hole, the peg needs to be a tight, secure, friction-fit.

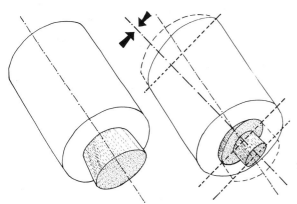

4 A piece at a time, mount the pegs in the wooden chuck, check that all is secure. Note the new angle and then turn off the shoulder and spigot.

2 Carefully check your wood for flaws, set it, a piece at a time, between centres and turn off a number of cones that are about 5 ins long, $2\frac{1}{4}$ ins at the base and taper to about $\frac{3}{4}$ in. Make a cone for each peg that you require.

3 With pencil, measure and callipers, mark off each peg so that the profile of the necked end is set out and established.

4 Set the wood up on a screw chuck, or a face plate and work the peg ends until they relate to the working drawings or your modified profile.

5 Work each peg to a good finish, aiming to make a matched set.

6 Mount a block of waste wood on the face plate and make a female chuck to take the pegs, work the tapered hole to a good, tight, friction-fit.

7 Remove the wooden chuck, cut its base at the same angle as the peg flange, establish the centre of the new peg tenon, knock off all sharp edges and then screw it back on the face plate.

8 Secure the wood, peg at time, in the chuck cone, then with great care turn off the base of each peg and work a flange and tenon.

9 Take each peg to a good finish and wax.

10 Set out and drill the rack plate, then glue, place and angle each peg.

Afterthoughts and modifications

This project, as with many others included in the book, can be made using a variety of methods. Adapt the project to suit your particular tools or requirements.

Each peg might have its own individually turned baseplate, rather than the pegs all being mounted on the same plate.

When you come to making the cone chuck, make sure that you cut back all potentially dangerous edges and corners.

For an insight into the origins and varieties of turned pegs, research into American Shaker furniture and fittings.

FOUR COLOUR GOBLET

Eric H. Ede

When Eric retired back in 1982, after a lifetime in the building industry, he purchased a new ELU DB180 lathe. Of course, as an apprenticed carpenter he had always enjoyed working with wood in all its forms, but now, at last, here was a chance to put his countryman's love for all things artistic into practice and create objects of beauty. At first his efforts were less than perfect, but with the encouragement of his wife and critic Margaret, and the help and advice of the newly formed Sussex Woodcraft Society, he soon began to develop unique woodturning skills. Members of the Society advised him as regards the purchase of exotic woods and friends passed on suitable off-cuts. Before his wife could say Chrysanthemum, he had made a series of goblets for her flower decorations! It didn't stop there, Eric soon wanted to explore new techniques and try something different, so he started experimenting with four-colour goblets, special chucks, home made clamps and other variations. Working in his small wooden workshop he now finds woodturning a totally absorbing hobby. His ambitions fulfilled, an active retirement and the support of a loving wife—what could be better?

LATHE TYPE
ELU DB180, with a patent ring chuck.

TOOLS AND MATERIALS
$1\frac{1}{4}$ in roughing-out gouge
1 in saw tooth machine bit
$\frac{1}{4}$ in, $\frac{3}{8}$ in and $\frac{3}{4}$ in spindle gouges
$\frac{3}{16}$ in fluted parting tool
you will also need:
a sanding sealer

small quantity of French polish
wax
wood glue
clamping jig

WOODS
Four 10 in lengths of $1\frac{1}{4}$ in square hardwood, walnut, mahogany, teak and beech.

What to do

1 Take the four lengths of wood, check them over for possible flaws, then carefully square each piece.

2 Look at the working drawings and the photograph on page 16, note the checkered end section, then glue and clamp the prepared wood to make a built-up piece that measures $2\frac{1}{2}$ ins square by 10 ins long. Note: the glued wood must be covered in newspaper or plastic film, prior to clamping/cramping to prevent wood-to-jig adhesion.

3 When the wood has been under pressure for at least three days, remove the clamps and leave it at room temperature for about 48 hours.

4 Place the wood between centres and turn a cylinder that fits your particular patent ring chuck.

5 Mount the chuck-secured cylinder of wood on the lathe, set the rest a little below centre and then true your blank so that it runs smoothly.

6 With gouge or drill, work a bowl–depth pilot hole.

7 Use a sawtooth machine bit to clear the waste

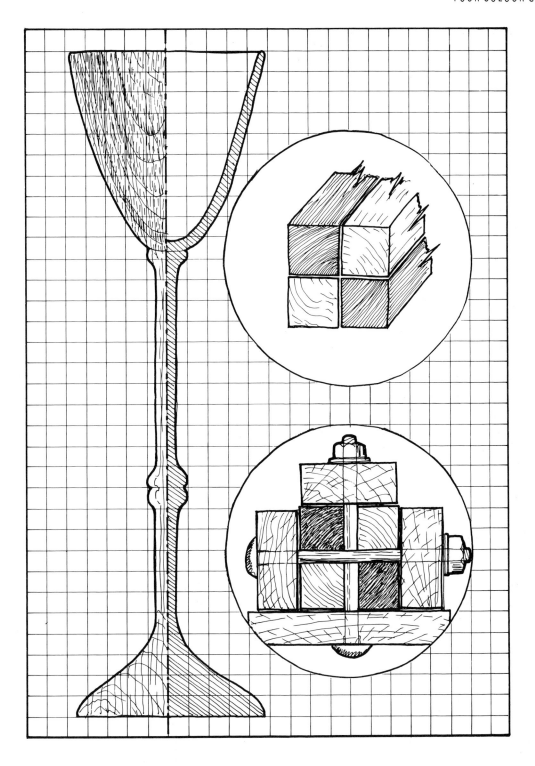

1 Working drawings. The scale is 1 grid square to $\frac{1}{4}$ in. Note the direction of the grain, and the quartered and coloured end section. See also the clamping jig detail.

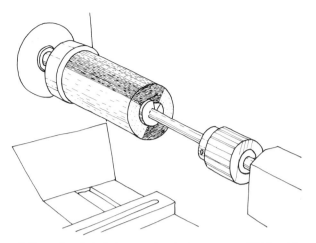

2 Secure the cylinder in the patent ring chuck, turn to a good finish and then use a sawtooth machine bit to clear away the bulk of the bowl waste.

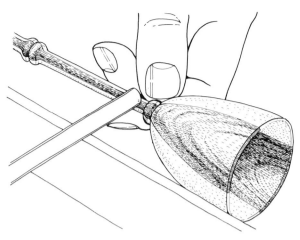

4 When you have worked the bowl and the foot, turn the stem to a good finish. To prevent whip, support the slender stem with one hand and control the tool with the other.

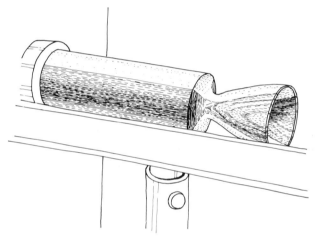

3 Once you have achieved a good inside bowl profile, clear away the waste from outside the bowl. Check wood thickness.

from inside the goblet bowl, and then with the tools of your choice work the bowl interior to a good finish.

8 Working with great care, clear the waste from around the body of the bowl and then with a great many checks, clear the wood until the bowl is the correct thickness.

9 When you have achieved what you consider to be a good bowl profile, strip away the main bulk of waste wood and reveal the goblet foot and stem.

10 Working with care and caution, support the delicate stem with one hand and control the tool with the other.

11 Finally, sand smooth and remove all the dust. Seal the grain, apply a thin coat of French polish and wax to a perfect finish. The goblet is now ready to be parted off the lathe.

Afterthoughts and modifications

If the stem whips, you can make a wooden plug and support the bowl with gentle pressure from the tailstock.

Clear the bowl waste with gouge and scraper, if you haven't got a sawtooth bit.

Before turning a goblet in an exotic wood, have a few trial dry runs with soft timber.

TWO-TIER CAKE STAND

Roger Marquand Farley

Roger enjoys wood-turning not only because he finds it relaxing and creative, but because of the immense pleasure it gives him when he makes presents for his family and friends. As to when Roger's interest in woodwork was first awakened, perhaps it has something to do with the fact that his father and grandfather before him were employed in the English 'round timber' trade. When he was married, in true pioneer spirit, Roger and his wife purchased a plot of land and built their own home. Of course by the time they had worked on everything from the skirting-boards to the wooden fixtures, Roger was a woodworker of no mean experience.

As a Telecom engineer, he visits all manner of people in their homes and from these refreshing encounters he draws the inspiration for many of his woodturning projects. His garage workshop is well equipped with a bandsaw, a radial arm saw, a 12 in circular saw, a planer, thicknesser and morticer, and a great many other small hand tools. When he settles down to turning, he doesn't draw out elaborate plans, instead he looks at his available wood, be it off-cuts or pieces that he has acquired from friends, and then he designs by eye, according to the size and character of the material.

What inspired this project? Picture in your minds eye Roger and his wife having Sunday tea in front of their open log fire, imagine the smell of the wood smoke, and culinary delights all beautifully set out—the cake stand is a one-off designed for just such an occasion.

LATHE TYPE
Myford ML8 with a $\frac{1}{2}$ HP motor and a selection of chucks.

TOOLS AND MATERIALS
roughing gouge
spindle gouge
skew chisel
selection of scraper tools (Roger made his from old files)
parting tool
internal and external callipers
compass
workout paper
graded pack of glass and garnet papers
wire wool
sealer

WOODS
You can use off-cuts of a wood type to suit. You need two 1 in thick blanks, one at 9 ins diameter and the other at $7\frac{1}{2}$ ins diameter. You also need two 7 in long pieces of $1\frac{1}{2} \times 1\frac{1}{2}$ in square-section timber, again of a type to suit.

What to do

1 Have a look at the working drawings and the photograph on page 24 and see how the stand is made up of four turnings, two plates, and a two-stage central handle or spindle. Note how the bottom spindle pierces the top plate and is then spigotted into the handle.

2 Mark out the 9 in diameter blank, screw it to a face plate, and then turn off the base, cut and work a foot ring that stands clear of the base by about $\frac{1}{16} - \frac{1}{8}$ in.

3 Mount a waster blank on the lathe, and then turn a face plate or dolly, work a recess to take the plate's foot ring.

4 When the plate is a secure and well mounted fit on the lathe, check the working drawings and

75

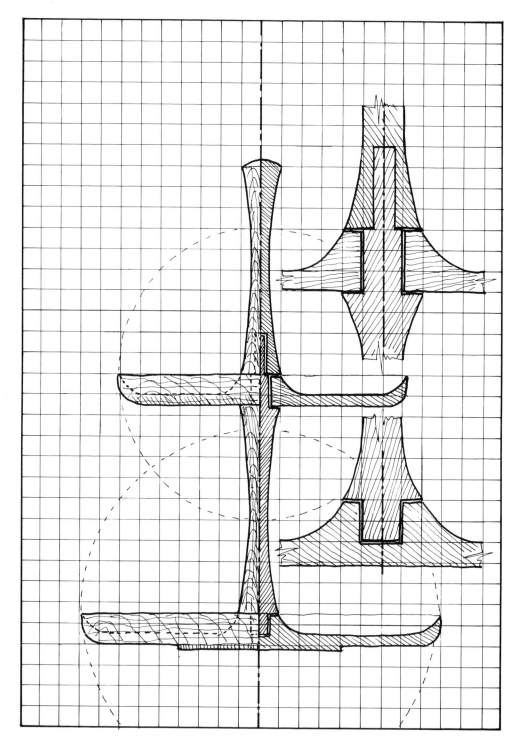

1 Working drawings. Centre left: the scale is 2 grid squares to 12 ins. Right: the details are worked to 4 grid squares to 1 in. See how the central shaft is placed through the top plate and spigotted into the handle. Note also the beautiful follow-through of the plates and the central shaft.

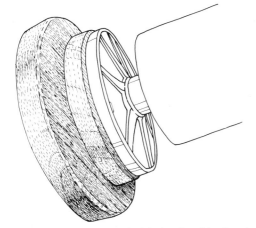

2 Make a wooden dolly or face plate to hold the foot ring of the plate, check that all is secure, and then turn off the plate's inside profile.

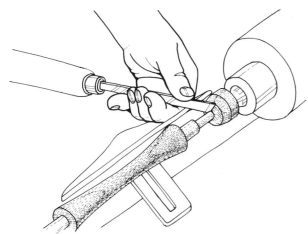

3 Turn the central shaft between centres, work a simple peg spigot on one end and a two-stage stepped spigot on the other.

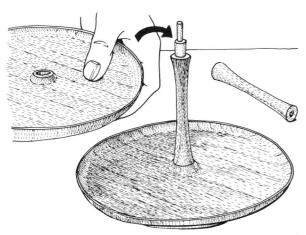

4 Glue the central shaft into the base plate, fit the top plate on the stepped spigot and finally fit and fix the handle. Note: before you put the project to one side to dry out, make sure all the parts are correctly aligned.

then turn off the inside profile of the plate to a good smooth-curved finish.

5 Note the flanged fit of the central spindle and work and drill the centre of the plate accordingly. Work a mortice or spigot hole that is about $\frac{1}{2}$ in deep and $\frac{1}{2}$ in diameter.

6 Now set about making the top plate in the same manner, this time mount the blank on a face plate and then a screw chuck.

7 Drill a $\frac{1}{2}$ in diameter hole through the centre of the upper $7\frac{1}{2}$ in diameter plate, and then bring both plates to a good finish.

8 Once complete, secure the $1\frac{1}{2}$ in square timber between centres, and turn off two near identical spindle shafts. Work one spindle so that it has a two-stage stepped spigot at one end and a $\frac{1}{2}$ in diameter spigot at the other. Work the other spindle so that it is domed at one end and drilled at the other (see the working drawing).

9 When all the turnings have been worked to a good fit and finish, clear the workbench of all dust and clutter, and set out the glue, the two plates and the two spindles.

10 Place, locate and glue the lower spindle into the base plate, fit and glue the top plate and then fit and fix the handle spindle. Check that the whole arrangement is square and well set up.

11 Finally, when the glue is dry, trim and make good and then polish with a dry duster.

Afterthoughts and modifications

The dishes can also be worked on an expanding collet chuck, or another special chuck. If you do decide to turn off a recess to take the lower plate's foot ring, ensure that the dolly and plate are a tight, secure friction-fit.

When you come to working the foot ring, make sure the base of the plate is left slightly concave in section.

When you are considering wood types, choose a close grained wood and avoid woods that have toxic or sticky characteristics.

LIGHTHOUSE LAMP

Mearns Nicoll Forge

The Isles of Islay and Stromness—the very names conjure up images of beautiful, far-away and romantic places. Well of course these places are not so beautiful, nor are they far away for Mearns, because he has worked for the Northern Lighthouse Service for nearly twenty years. Joiner, boat builder and now lighthouse keeper,

he has always enjoyed working with wood and he particularly finds woodturning an adventurous and inspirational craft. Most of his projects start as vague ideas, ideas which gradually take shape as he sketches them out on scraps of paper and spends time considering all the design and working implications. His workshop is usually on the station premises, so there is plenty of room, and, as you can imagine, lots of interesting scraps of wood.

This project is his most adventurous to date and it was inspired by an actual lighthouse paraffin vapour lamp that was designed in 1901. There are two of these still in use in the service, the rest made obsolete by the introduction of gas and electric lights.

Working alternate months, it helps if Rock Keepers have as many hobbies and interests as possible. Building model clinker boats, woodcarving, painting watercolours, woodturning all in addition to being a lighthouse keeper suggests that Mearns is always ready to take on any new art or craft venture. He is a man in a unique and perhaps enviable position.

LATHE TYPE
A twenty year old Black and Decker drill lathe with a speed reducer and a selection of chucks.

TOOLS AND MATERIALS
$\frac{1}{2}$ in gouge
$\frac{3}{4}$ in skew chisel
$\frac{3}{4}$ in parting tool
spoon-shaped chisel
Hegner multi-cut fret saw
callipers
pencil

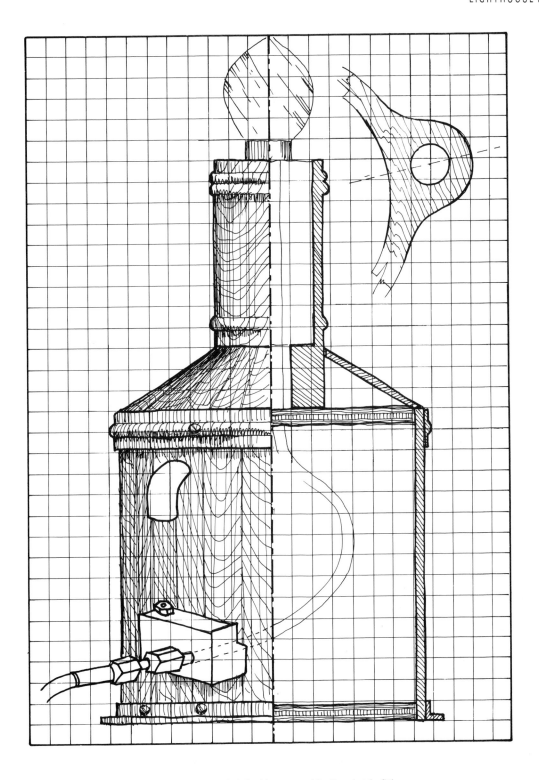

1 Working drawings. The scale is 4 grid squares to 1 in. Note that the fittings are not drawn to scale. See how the structure is coopered and built around two plywood discs and a centrally placed, turned lampholder.

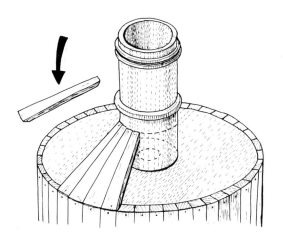

2 Place the turned lampholder so that it is centred on the top most pierced disc, then build up the barrel form using staves. Note: before turning off to a good finish, ensure that all the pin heads are punched well below the surface of the wood.

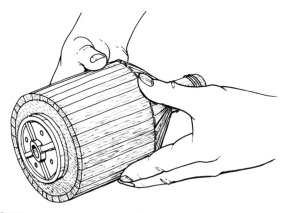

3 When you have pinned and glued the coopered form, mount it on a face plate and turn to round.

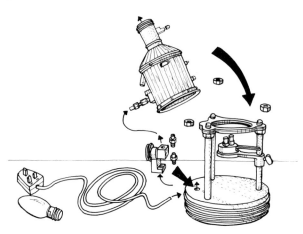

4 Once you have achieved the main structure, fit, fix and glue the various small turnings. Notice how the electrical flex doubles up as a gas tube look-a-like.

measure
workout paper
graded glass paper
polyurethane varnish
various other small tools

WOODS
Strips of mahogany, dowel rod and off-cuts of beech, ramin and plywood.

What to do

1 Before you start this project, be prepared to spend some time considering the working methods in general and the design in particular. Do you want to make an exact copy of this lamp? Or do you perhaps want to modify the details and make a lamp which is more familiar to you—a model of a Victorian oil lamp or an Edwardian carriage lamp.

2 When you have a clear picture in your mind of how you want your lamp to be, then take a pencil and workout paper and draw up a full set of measured drawings. Consider how the body of the lamp is to be coopered from mahogany staves and how all the details, the wick holder and the nuts and fittings are turned, carved and worked in ramin and beech.

3 Start by turning the $2\frac{1}{4}$ in high bulb mount, work between centres, or with a chuck special, and turn off a cylinder that has a recess for the bulb and a shop-bought bulb holder. Note the $\frac{1}{2}$ in hole for the electric flex.

4 When you have achieved a well finished, cylindrical form, put it to one side and then use a coping or fret saw, and perhaps the lathe, to cut and work the two large $\frac{3}{8}$ in thick plywood discs. Note: the top disc needs to be pierced.

5 Pin and fix the lamp holder so that it is centred over the pierced disc, then, using the $\frac{1}{8}$ in thick staves, begin to build up the barrel-like form.

6 When you have fixed and fitted all the staves, and generally framed up the form, mount the whole thing on the lathe, and turn off all the stave facets.

7 When the stave-built cylinder has been well turned and finished, cut, trim and fit the top strap and the bottom flange rings, then go back to the lathe and turn off the decorative ring profiles.

8 When you have achieved the main body of the lamp, mount a 2 in thick, 8 in diameter mahogany blank on the lathe and turn off the ring-decorated base.

9 Finally, turn off all the little fittings. Use a fret or coping saw to work the various non-turned pieces, place, glue and fit and then take the whole project to a smooth, well rubbed down and varnished finish.

Afterthoughts and modifications

Mearns, naturally enough, has drawn inspiration from his understanding of a particular type of lighthouse lamp, he is familiar with its form and workings. You, on the other hand might be a railway buff, a canal enthusiast or whatever, in which case you would choose to make say a locomotive lamp or a narrow-boat lamp. Stay with the general working methods, but if possible relate this project to a form or object with which you are familiar.

In many ways, with a project of this character, it is better to design the fittings and fixtures as the work progresses.

When you have pinned, glued, and built up the coopered form, make sure that you punch in the pins before turning off.

PAIR OF VASES

Adran Franklin

Adran had always been interested in art and design, and so when he left school, he decided to work in the printing trade. However, after five years with the same firm, he felt that it was time to move on and broaden his horizons. It was about this time, after visiting a friend's workshop, that he first became interested in woodworking and turning, 'he asked me if I would like to have a go . . . gave me a block of walnut, told me a few hints, and from then on I was addicted . . .' From that day to this, Adran has been looking around for fresh woodturning ideas, new forms, and different methods of working.

Although in many ways he finds woodturning limiting, he also considers that it is perhaps these very limitations that make woodturning an exciting and challenging craft.

When Adran came to designing this particular project, he had in mind a great many rather sad 'lonely' little bowls that he has seen over the years, and thought that making two identical well balanced forms on his small lathe would be a challenging prospect. Most of his wood is 'found'. This process of searching around for wood and then using say a scrap of salvaged timber with unknown qualities, only adds spice to what is already a stimulating craft. Taking the wood back to the workshop, converting it for the lathe and then exploring the creative and artistic potential offered by the craft—Adran enjoys the whole wonderful and exciting experience.

LATHE TYPE
Coronet Minor with a 1 HP motor and various chucks.

TOOLS AND MATERIALS
small round nose gouge
round nose scraper
parting tools
callipers
pencil
measure
workout paper
polyurethane varnish
spray gun (optional)
wax
an inner water vessel (see the working drawings)
graded glasspapers
and all the usual workshop tools and materials

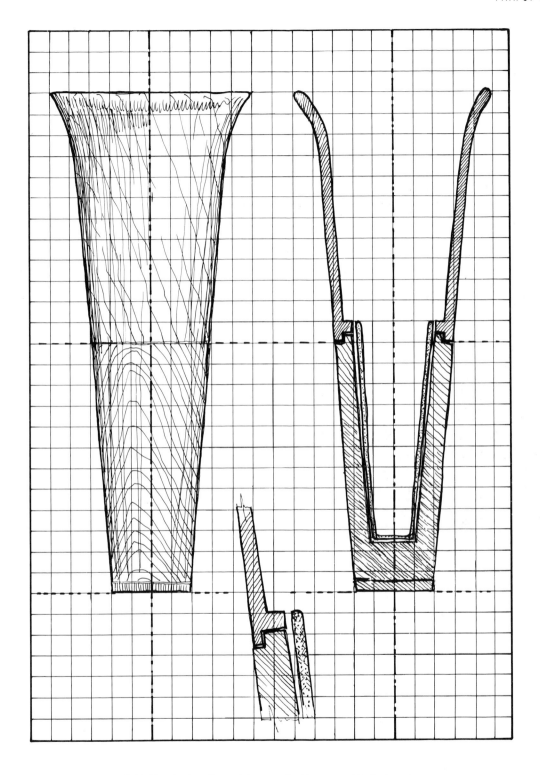

1 Working drawings. The scale is approx. 2 grid squares to 1 in. See how the vase is made up from three turnings and how the project needs to be designed around an inner water-tight vessel.

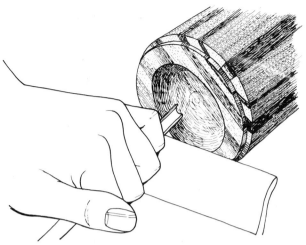

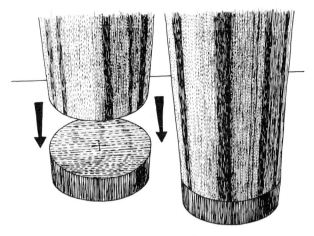

2 Mount the rosewood blank on the lathe and turn off a slightly tapered form, work the square-cut stepped rim and turn out the interior so that the water vessel is an easy sliding fit.

4 Finally, fit and glue the lignum vitae base disc in position and work to a smooth finish.

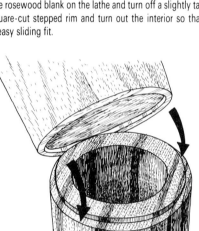

3 Check that the two turnings come together for a good fit.

WOODS

Oak for the upper half of the vase (Adran used oak salvaged from a gate post), rosewood for the lower half, and lignum vitae for the base disc.

What to do

1 Have a look at the working drawings and see how the whole project relates to an inner water-tight vessel. The vessel might be plastic, glass or whatever, as long as it's slender and conical.

2 When you have found a suitable water-tight inner container, go back to the working draw-ings and see how the turned form is built up from three pieces of wood. Note: it is very important at this stage, that you appreciate just how the vase might be built-up and worked. For example you could glue the three pieces of wood together and then use a chuck special, or you could work the wood in stages and then glue it together, and so on.

3 When you have considered all the possible working methods, take your three pieces of prepared wood and mark them out accordingly.

4 Using the chuck of your choice, take the piece of prepared rosewood and mount it on the lathe.

5 With a measure, callipers and the tools of your choice, turn off a nicely considered tapered form, turn the interior and work the square-cut stepped rim.

6 When you have achieved a good form and the water–tight vessel is a loose slide-fit, take the wood to a smooth finish and take it off the lathe.

7 Mount the prepared oak blank and using your rosewood base as a template/guide, cut and work the base-to-rim stepped joint.

8 Now check that the oak and the rosewood come together for a good fit, then glue and clamp up.

9 Using one or other of the chucking methods, put the partially worked wood back on the lathe, make sure that the wood is secure and then start to turn and hollow the top half of the vase.

10 Run the turning tool through the oak and continue until you have pierced the top half of the vase.

11 When you have cut through the oak, use callipers and the tools of your choice to establish and work both the interior and the rim.

12 Turn off the form so that the two halves/woods run together as one.

13 When you have worked the wood to a good finish, take the vase from the lathe, and turn off the little lignum vitae base disc.

14 Finally, glue-mount the base to the vase, work the whole to a good finish and the job is done.

Afterthoughts and modifications

Before you start this project you must consider all the working methods and then plan your working order accordingly.

When you are choosing your wood, try if possible to choose wood types that have the same shrinkage and working characteristics and reject material that looks warped or split.

MINER'S LAMP

Anthony Gill

Tony has been woodturning for around 20 years, and during this time he made everything from working spinning wheels and curtain poles, to barometers, and, of course, miners' lamps. He has spent most of his life underground working for the Coal Board, recently as a Deputy, so the amount of time devoted to woodturning has been limited. However, since entering the *Practical Woodworking* Woodturning competition, he has been made redundant. Is Tony heartbroken, depressed, bored, missing the coal dust, and longing to get back to the daily sweat and toil? Not at all, he is now spending nearly all his time woodturning, and loving every moment of it.

His lathe is an old metal turning machine with a 1 HP motor, a 9 in swing, and an outboard that allows him to turn 20 in diameter spinning wheel rims. He uses four face plates, a couple of combination chucks and a very useful multi-purpose chuck with an expanding collet. For wood, he turns just about everything that he can lay his hands on, pieces that are begged and borrowed, bits that he reclaims from demolition sites, they are all grist to Tony's woodturning mill!

As for designs and project ideas, he tends to take them from his immediate surroundings, for example with this particular project he drew his inspiration directly from his collection of miners' lamps. Before he starts work on the lathe, Tony spends quite some time making jigs and templates, but he finds that this pre-lathe preparation speeds up the job, and contributes to a better end product. A one-time miner, and now a full-time part-time woodturner, if you see what I mean! Tony is having a great time.

LATHE TYPE

An old metal lathe with a 1 HP motor, an inboard with a 9 in swing and a 20 in diameter outboard and a full range of chucks.

TOOLS AND MATERIALS

1 in parting chisel
1 in gouge
$\frac{1}{2}$ in flat chisel (used on its side)
workout paper
pencil and measure
wire wool
varnish
wax
template card
scissors
and the usual workshop tools and materials

WOODS

For this project you need two pieces of mahogany, one at $6 \times 4 \times 4$ ins, and the other at $4 \times 4 \times 4$ ins. You also need five 4 in lengths of $\frac{1}{4}$ in dowel. Note: The trim, ring and glass can be obtained from The Miners' Lamp manufacturers (an acrylic glass dealer will also supply the glass), and the badge can be obtained from a trophy shop.

What to do

1 Have a good look at the working drawings and the photograph on page 10 and see how the project is made up from two turnings, the uppermost 'bonnet', and the lower 'vessel'. See also how there are five dowels set apart at an angle of 72°, a tube-lined wick hole and a glass wick cover.

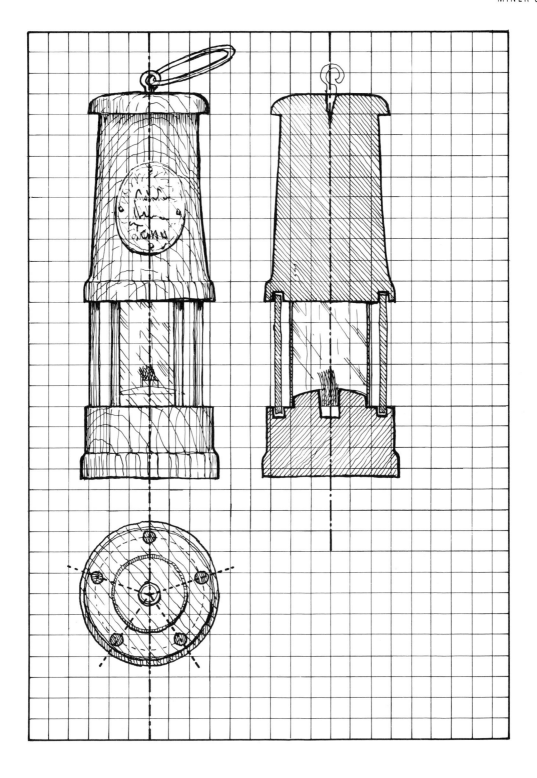

1 Working drawings. The scale is 2 grid squares to 1 in. The lamp is built up from two solid turnings, and five dowels.

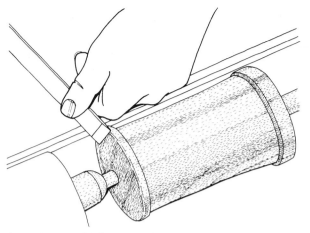

2 It might be as well, before you start this project to visit a museum and have a look at a miner's lamp in the flesh, as it were. For an authentic lamp it is important that the bonnet has just the right taper and feel.

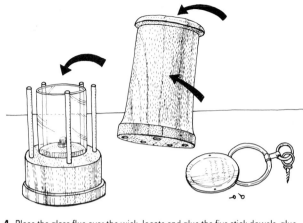

4 Place the glass flue over the wick, locate and glue the five stick dowels, glue all the holes, fit the bonnet and finally trim and finish.

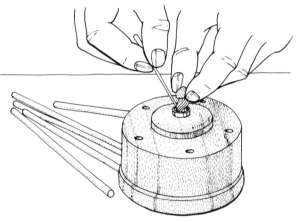

3 When you have turned off the vessel, fix and fit a short length of metal tube and then place within and glue an inch or so of wick.

2 When you have had a good look at the project and considered all the design implications, then settle down with the workout paper and a pencil, and finalize the details.

3 Mount the $6 \times 4 \times 4$ in piece of mahogany between centres, and turn off a cylinder that is about 3 ins in diameter.

4 Note the depth and diameter of the bonnet cap, and then taper and cut-in accordingly, try to achieve the authentic profile.

5 When the bonnet has been turned, worked to a good finish and parted off, then set the other piece of mahogany between centres and turn off a $3\frac{1}{2}$ in diameter cylinder.

6 Using a template, and the tools of your choice, turn off all the lips and steps that go to make up the vessel's profile.

7 Cut back the wick mounting so that the flue glass can be slid onto the stepped wick dome and then take the wood to a good finish.

8 Rub down with wire wool, and then lay on three coats of varnish, rub down between coats.

9 Set out the position of the ten $\frac{1}{4}$ in dowel holes, five in the bonnet and five in the vessel, and then work the holes so that they are about $\frac{1}{4}$ in deep.

10 Drill out a $\frac{1}{2}$ in diameter wick hole, line it with a short length of copper or stainless steel tube, and then place and stick the short length of wick into position.

11 Clear the workbench of all dust, and set out the parts of the lamp.

12 Place the glass flue over the wick dome, fit and glue the five dowels into the vessel holes, place and glue the tops of the dowels into the bonnet and make sure that the project is well aligned.

13 Finally, screw on the little bonnet ring, fit

the presentation badge, rub the whole thing down with a smooth cloth and the job is done.

Afterthoughts and modifications

The bonnet is solid, the project might perhaps be modified so that the bonnet is hollow worked.

Tony has modified one or two of these lamps and made table lighters and other variations on a theme of which there are numerous possibilities.

Similar badges, to those used in the project, can be obtained at sports and trophy shops. If you do decide to make a presentation piece, do not forget to sign and date the base.

JEWELLERY DISPLAY TRAY

George William Henry Graham

Bill, a centre lathe and general metal turner by profession, has a small compact workshop well set out with lathes, one for metal and two for wood. Until about four years ago he had only 'messed about' and made various lathe fittings and tools—chucks, chisels, and such like. He only started woodturning seriously after attending a seminar at 'The Mill' in Buxton. A few sessions with Ray Kay and Mick O'Donnel, and he was well and truely hooked. At work he's on batch production, so when he comes home and settles down to a bit of relaxing woodturning on his home made lathe, his projects tend to be one

offs. So far Bill has attended two craft shows, of course he plans to do more, but its got to be said that he doesn't relish the thought of turning off batch quantities.

When it comes to designing, Bill usually draws his inspiration directly from other media craft sources. He starts a project by playing around with a general idea, such as a glass dish, or a ceramic bowl, and then he tries to develop and extend the original and follow it through in wood. The idea for the jewellery tray came to him when he was looking through his son's geometry book and spotted a section on cones

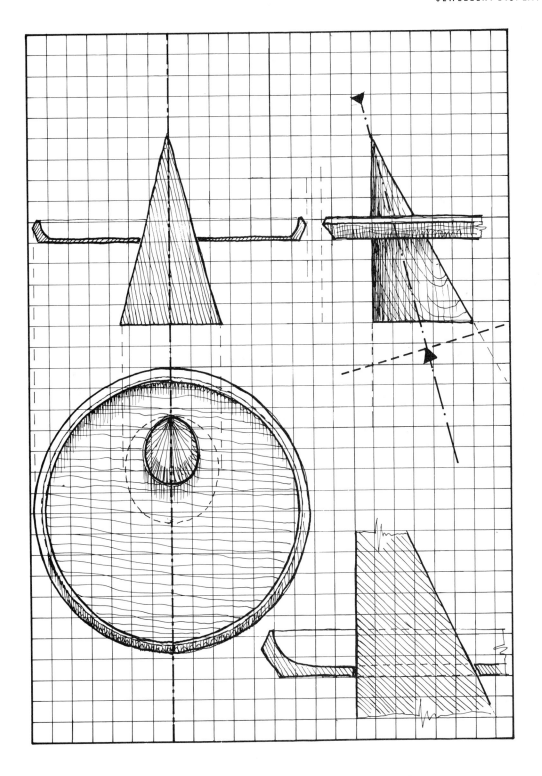

1 Working drawings. The scale is 2 grid squares to 1 in. See how a true cone is worked between centres and then base angled. Note how the wood thickness around the circumference of the tray hole is variously angled to fit the cone.

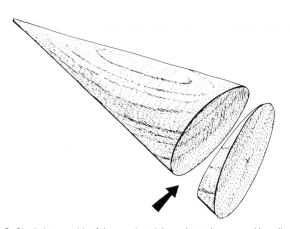

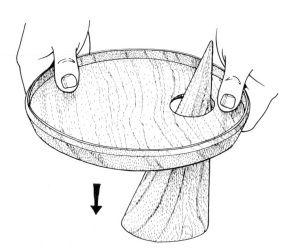

2 Check that one side of the cone is at right angles to the proposed base line, then cut and size the cone to suit.

4 Noting the angle of the cone to base, mount the tray on a wedge face plate and cut the tapered off-centre cone hole. This operation is rather tricky, so if in doubt, turn off a couple of scrap wood prototypes.

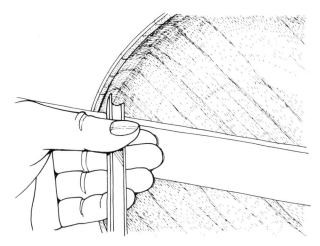

3 Mount a blank on the lathe and turn off a shallow dish tray, aim to achieve a delicate rim and lip.

TOOLS AND MATERIALS
$\frac{1}{2}$ in spindle gouge
$1\frac{1}{2}$ in skew chisel
$\frac{1}{2}$ in bowl gouge
HSS scraper
special angled plate/chuck
special angled guide/rest to cut the tapered dish hole
band saw
sanding sealer
quick drying wax paste
graded glass paper
and all the usual small tools and materials

WOODS
Elm for the tray, laburnum for the cone, and scrap wood for the prototype.

and elipses. As to why he entered this competition, it's simple enough—he knows his wife and family like everything that he makes, but then they would wouldn't they! Bill just wanted to find out how his work measured up to that of other crafters and turners.

LATHE TYPE
Home made lathe, to roughly the same specifications as the Harrison Graduate, with a 1 HP motor, a 15 in swing overboard, 36 ins between centres, 24 in swing outboard and double taper adjustable roller bearings.

What to do
1 First have a look at the working drawings and a check through the tool list. See how Bill has used his metal turning know-how to make and use special chucks and plates, because of this, you will need to devise an angled dish mount or modify the design. It might be helpful to make a prototype.

2 When you have a clear understanding of how

the project is to be worked, mark out your wood and set out your tools and materials.

3 Mount the laburnum on the lathe and turn off a cone using heart wood and cutting through while checking the working drawing for the cone angle and dimensions. Take the cone to a good form and finish.

4 When you have achieved what you consider to be a good conical form, remove the work from the lathe, note the finished height and base dimensions, check that one side of the cone is at 90° to the proposed base line and then use a bandsaw to cut the cone to size.

5 Mount the elm on the lathe using a face plate or a chuck special and then turn off a shallow, well considered dish form which is the tray. Note the delicate rim and lip feature.

6 When you have taken the tray to a good finish, mount it on an angled face plate and then cut and turn a tapered, off-centre hole.

7 Finally, when you have turned off both the tray and the cone, have made good and taken the wood to a fine finish, then the two forms can be put together.

Afterthoughts and modifications

This project is a bit tricky because Bill uses several home made, special tools—an angled face plate and a turning tool. You might decide to cut and work the tray hole using the trial and error approach, if you do, cut yourself a hole template.

If you do decide to make and use an angled/wedged face plate when cutting the hole, watch out for the off-centre swing of the tray rim.

When you are choosing your wood, avoid bits that appear stained, split or have dead knots, and, most important of all, make sure that the wood you use for the tray is unwarped.

BOWL IN MAHOGANY AND SYCAMORE

Derek Greenacre

A teacher in middle school, Derek likes making things, and finds woodturning one of the more satisfying aspects of this pleasure. His 8 ft square workshop is packed with items which 'may be useful at some later date'. But pride of place is his five year old Coronet 'Elf' lathe. It has a longer than standard bed so that he can work 3 ft between centres.

A man of many interests (most of them outdoor), Derek tends to work on the lathe only when the weather is bad. Designs are rarely repeated. Usually he starts a project with a general idea and then develops it as he goes

along. However, there are projects that need careful pre-lathe planning, and when this is the case, he painstakingly draws out designs and cuts out templates. As for materials he may buy exotic woods specially or use off-cuts, depending on the nature of the work.

As a general approach to turning, Derek feels that a piece of character wood, that is to say a wood with a good grain, needs nothing more than to be worked with sensitivity to the material. When the grain is not enough in itself, then, as with this project, he likes to combine wood types to create a dynamic effect. Derek's

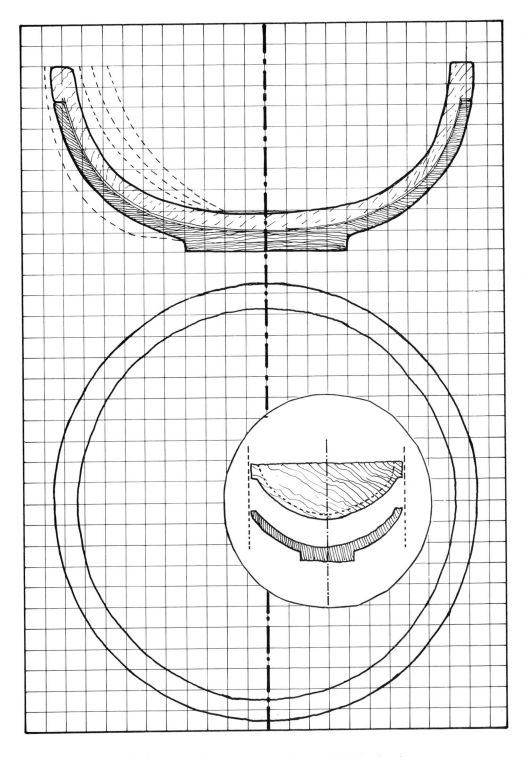

1 Working drawings. The scale is approx. 4 grid squares to 1 in. Note how the project consists of a mahogany outer bowl which is lined with a sycamore inner. See how the double thickness of sycamore at the rim is an important design feature.

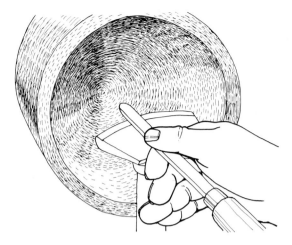

2 Screw the prepared mahogany blank to the face plate and establish a good clean interior.

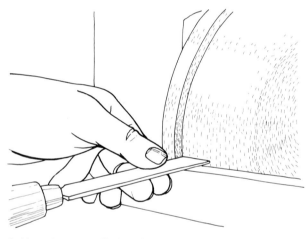

3 Mount the sycamore blank on the lathe, and then with the tools of your choice, work a convex form that fits within the mahogany outer bowl. Pay particular attention to the rim, leave it square-cut.

4 Fit and glue the sycamore blank inside the mahogany outer bowl, then work as with a straight forward turning.

woodturning design philosophy can be summed up by the old adage 'if it looks right, then it is right'.

LATHE TYPE
A Coronet 'Elf' with a longer than standard bed.

TOOLS AND MATERIALS
$\frac{1}{2}$ in long and strong gouge
$\frac{3}{4}$ in skew chisel
$\frac{1}{2}$ in scraper
small quantitiy of wood glue

grain filler
wax and polish
template card
scissors
compass
pencil
callipers
measure
and of course you will also need all the usual workshop items

WOODS
A piece of mahogany that measures about $6 \times 6 \times 3$ ins and a piece of sycamore of the same dimensions.

What to do
1 First take a good long look at the working drawings and the photograph. See how the two wood types have been combined to make the bowl and note how, at the rim, the sycamore liner laps over the mahogany outer bowl.

2 Make sure your wood is flawless then set out the prepared block of mahogany and screw it to a face plate or screw chuck.

3 With the full range of tools, turn off the inner and outer profiles, aim to leave the underside of the rim square and sharp edged.

4 Remove the mahogany outer bowl from the lathe, then set out the prepared block of sycamore and secure it to the face plate or screw chuck.

5 With a template, callipers and the full range of tools, turn off a smooth-curved convex form. Work the sycamore until it's a snug fit at base and rim within the mahogany outer bowl.

6 Check that the male/female fit of the two forms, is as illustrated, then glue the two together.

7 When the glue is dry, screw the base of the mahogany bowl to the face plate and with great care start to turn out the inner sycamore profile.

8 Keeping one eye on the working drawings and your various templates always at hand, gradually turn the bowl interior down to the required depth.

9 Turn off the inner sycamore layer so that it also forms the rim or lip of the bowl.

10 Work both the sycamore liner and the mahogany outer bowl until they run together as a single, well-considered whole.

11 Finally, when you have achieved what you consider to be a good form, work to a good finish, brush on two coats of grain filler, clear away all the dust and clutter, and then polish.

Afterthoughts and modifications

You could use a face plate, a screw chuck or one of the patent chucks.

Change the order of working and turn the inner form first if you prefer.

If you do decide to make this project, but would like to use other wood types, check that they have the same shrinkage, design and behavioural characteristics.

When working the inner and outer bowls, use callipers and templates and as you turn the two layers closer to their limits, keep taking calliper readings.

When you are choosing the two wood types, check that they are, more or less, equally seasoned.

BABY'S RATTLE

Reginald Hamley

Reg has been interested in woodwork ever since the tender age of 11 when he was given a fretwork outfit for a Christmas present. Over the years and prior to going to University, he made a number of fretwork items, but apart from household DIY, his woodworking activities tended to decline. However, over the last five years or so, he has 'gone back into production', making all manner of items for church and R.S.P.B. bazaars. Standing at 5 ft 6 in, his 5 ft 5 ft 7 in high cellar might well have been designed for him, it makes the perfect workshop. As for woodturning, he really began about three years ago when he purchased a lathe attachment for his Black and Decker drills. I say drills, because he has one permanently attached to an orbital sander, another is used to power a table saw, a variable speed drill is used to power his lathe and Hobbies Gem Treadle Fretsaw, and yet another is kept in the vertical drill stand.

Reg is a man of many parts—designer, woodturner, and winner of a Gold Award in the toy section, at the 1985 Bristol Woodworker Show. He finds woodworking a pleasant relaxation, very different from his full-time job of teaching mathematics, statistics and computer studies in a comprehensive school.

LATHE TYPE
An electric drill, D77–H17 with a Black and Decker attachment D944, and a screw chuck.

TOOLS AND MATERIALS
$\frac{1}{2}$ in skew chisel
$\frac{3}{8}$ in gouge
callipers
measure
pencil
3 drill bits with diameters of $1\frac{1}{2}$ in, $\frac{1}{2}$ in and $\frac{1}{4}$ in
small quantity of wood glue

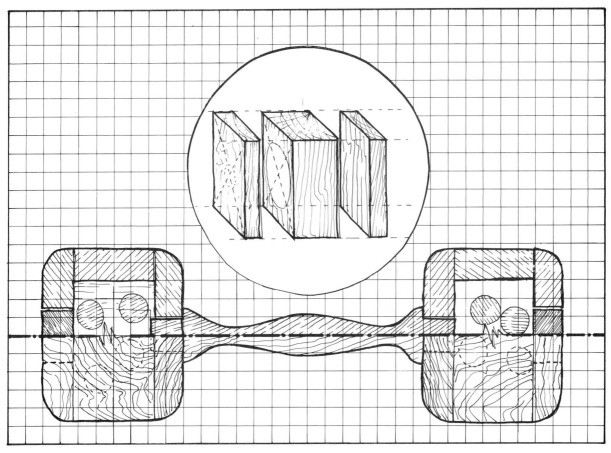

1 Working drawings. The scale is 4 grid squares to 1 in. Note how the spindle is plugged into the two little bead boxes and how the chuck holes are plugged with a contrasting wood.

workout paper
sanding sealer
polishing wax

WOODS
Small off-cuts of mahogany and beech. Check that your wood is splinter resistant and non-toxic.

What to do

1 Have a good look at the working drawings and see how the rattle is built up from four pieces of mahogany of about $2\frac{1}{2} \times 2\frac{1}{2} \times \frac{1}{2}$ ins, two pieces of mahogany of about $2\frac{1}{2} \times 2\frac{1}{2} \times 1\frac{1}{4}$ ins, a single piece of beech about $4\frac{1}{2}$ ins long and 1×1 in square and eight plastic or wooden beads.

2 When you have studied the various drawings and photographs, adjust and modify the project to suit, then draw up a series of design sketches.

3 Take the two thick blocks of mahogany, find the centres and bore a $1\frac{1}{2}$ in diameter hole through each.

4 Carefully glue and position the thin pieces of mahogany over the 2 drilled blocks, check that all is correct, then clamp up.

5 When the glue has hardened, take the wood, a block at a time, find the centre and mount it on a screw or special chuck.

6 Turn the wood down to a $2\frac{3}{8}$ in diameter cylinder and delicately turn off the sharp leading edge leaving it rounded.

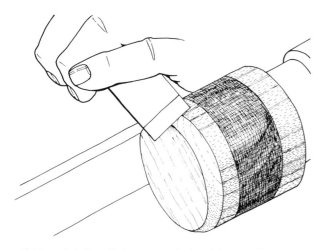

2 Mount the built-up block on a screw chuck, and then turn off the little pill-box form.

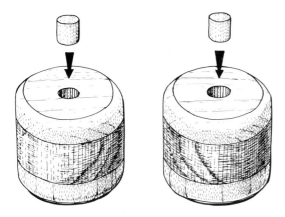

3 On each of the boxes, cut, plug and handwork one of the chuck-screw holes and treat it as a decorative feature.

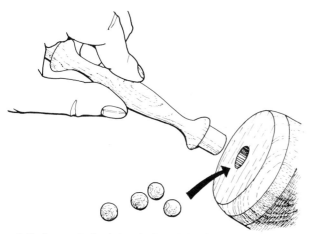

4 Finally, pop the beads into the little pill-box forms, and then glue the spindle-shaft into place.

7 Reverse the cylinder on the screw chuck and turn off the opposite end to match, do this with both blocks.

8 Aim to turn both close-end cylinders down to small pill box forms, then bring to a fine finish and polish with beeswax.

9 Now drill out the chuck-screw holes in both cylinders, work the cylinders so that each has two holes, one at about $\frac{1}{2}$ in diameter and the other at about $\frac{3}{4}$ in diameter.

10 Cut, plug and handwork the smaller of the two holes, use a matching or a contrasting wood to make the plugged hole a decorative feature.

11 Turn the beech wood between centres and work a nicely curved spindle bar.

12 Turn $\frac{1}{2}$ in diameter spigots on the bar ends and work a flange.

13 Bring the linking bar to a fine finish with beeswax polish and then part off.

14 Pop three or four wooden beads into each of the two pill-box cylinders, then glue, fit and clamp the connecting bar and bring the whole to a good finish with a light coat of wax and a soft, fluff-free cloth.

Afterthoughts and modifications

If you do decide to modify this project remember that the cylinder ends need to be safe and baby-proof in terms of wood type and size. The cylinders must be made of non-toxic wood, the wood must be splinter resistant, and the cylinders must be bigger than a baby's mouth!

The project could be adjusted so that the spigot ends go right through the cylinder.

The linking spindle needs to be baby-hand size, but at the same time it must be strong and snap–proof.

LATHE BIRD

Ivan Harrington

Ivan started woodturning again in 1984 when his son wanted a lathe for Christmas. He had done quite a bit of turning in the past on his parents' small farm when he was a young man in the early '50s. When he married and had a home of his own, he set up his own workshop.

Now, apart from the lathe which really belongs to his son, he has a steel framed circular saw with a rise and fall table, which he built himself, a bandsaw made from steel plate and scrap, which he also built, a 6 in planing machine, a treadle fretsaw, a hand bench drill, and a deal of other joinery and engineering tools. As to what inspired Ivan to make the Lathe Bird, he isn't really sure, but thinks that he was probably trying to come up with an idea to challenge his son who is now turning out some excellent items himself.

Ivan gets his wood from friends who own or work in joinery shops. They are generally off-cuts or plank ends of mahogany, ash, iroko, elm, afrormosia, oak, teak, luan and pine. Since entering the competition Ivan has gone on to make a number of variations on the Lathe Bird.

LATHE TYPE
ELU DB180 with various chucks.

TOOLS AND MATERIALS
Sorby skew chisel
$\frac{1}{2}$ in and $\frac{3}{4}$ in Taylor scrapers
gloss varnish
fretsaw or coping saw
short length of wire for the legs
callipers
measure
pencil

workout paper
pins and glue
and all the usual workshop tools

WOOD
Small off-cuts of mahogany.

What to do

1 Have a look at the working drawings and photographs and see how the bird is made up from two turnings—a head and a body. Note also how the wings are cut and worked from flat wood.

2 When you have a clear understanding of how the various parts of the bird are to be cut and

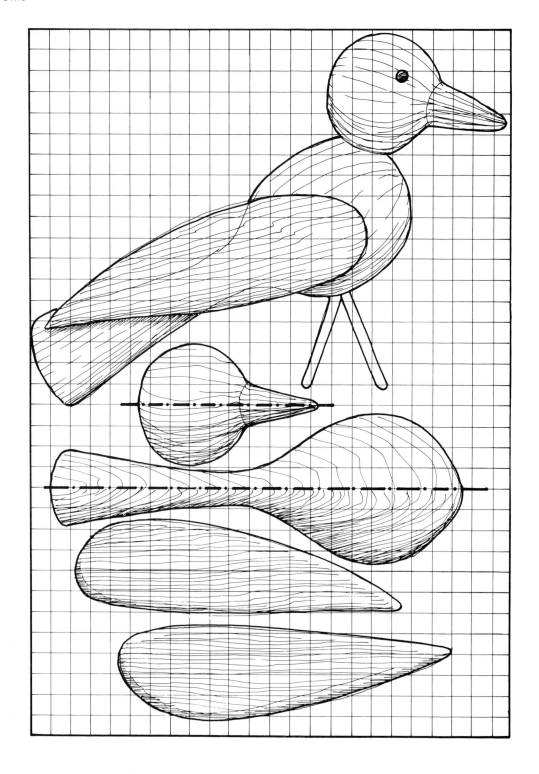

1 Working drawings. The scale is approx. 4 grid squares to 1 in. Note the angle at which the head and the wings are fixed to the body and how the wire legs are angled and spread.

worked, fit a length of mahogany to the screw chuck and start turning off a long cylinder.

3 With the tools of your choice, turn the head-and-beak (remove the tailstock in order to finish the beak), check the overall form against your working drawings and then part off.

4 Once the head has been made and cut off from the cylinder, move the tailstock up and start shaping the bird's body.

5 Turn the body-and-tail, check with your working drawings again and then part off.

6 The head can now be fixed to the body. Use the threaded end cut from a wood screw and secure with a small amount of wood glue. The bird, beak-to-tail should now measure about $4\frac{1}{2}$ ins.

7 Take a piece of mahogany, use a fretsaw to cut a couple of thin slices, then cut and work two identical wing profiles.

8 Position, glue and pin the wings to the body, drill and plug the wire legs to the underside of the body, dab in the eyes with a small paint brush, bring the whole to a good finish and brush on two or three coats of clear gloss varnish.

9 Finally, search around for a wood-in-bark base and mount the bird to suit.

Afterthoughts and modifications

If you require the bird's wings to match the body, cut the thin slices for the wings off the same piece of wood that is going to be used for the body, using a circular saw or bandsaw.

The head could be dowel-fixed to the body, rather than screwed.

The wings might better be dowel-fixed to the body and the dowel ends worked as a design feature.

The eyes might be established with brass pins or dowels rather than painted.

The wings could be made from a contrasting wood and perhaps also textured.

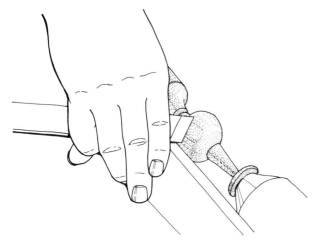

2 Secure the wood between centres and then turn off the various parts, the head, and the body-and-tail. You might at this stage modify the turnings to suit.

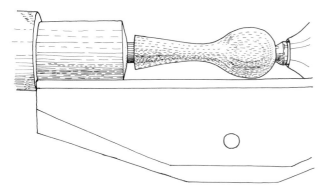

3 The body-and-tail need to be considered as an integral form, you might need to work several prototypes before you get it just right.

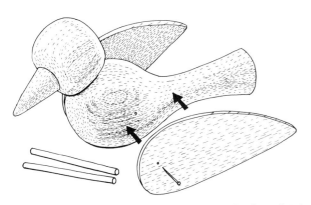

4 The head is plugged and screw-mounted using either a dowel or a clipped wood screw, and the wings are pinned. The dowels could be considered as a design feature if worked in contrasting wood.

BOX FOR COLOUR SLIDES

J. Michael Hold

Michael, better known as Mike, is interested in general woodwork, his current projects ranging from a summer house to small turned objects. His workshop is a large garage below the living room, very convenient and nicely warmed by the central heating boiler. His approach to design varies widely, sometimes he makes working drawings and protoypes, and other times just puts a piece of wood on the lathe and shapes it as the mood takes him. With the slide box project, he spent a great deal of time considering possible forms, then he drew up measured designs and finalized the details by turning off a prototype. Mike thinks that his 20 year career in the analysis and design of computer based information systems industry, plus his current experience as a Polytechnic lecturer, have led him to adopt his flexible, multi-design approach.

He gets his wood from a variety of sources. In this case the sycamore came from a local yard where it had been put aside for use as a butcher's cutting block. Mike intends this box to be the first of many, the next will be designed for the storage of computer discs. What inspired Mike? Perhaps it was the challenge, or the thought of the prize money, or maybe it was just the joy and satisfaction of working the wood ... who knows?

LATHE TYPE
Tyme Cub with a $\frac{1}{2}$ HP motor.

TOOLS AND MATERIALS
$\frac{3}{4}$ in skew chisel
roughing gouge
round-nosed scraper
router and jig
saw
workout paper
linseed oil
and all the usual general workshop tools and materials

WOOD
A quantity of spalted sycamore—amount to suit the project.

What to do

1 Have a good look at the working drawings and the photograph on page 19. Then modify the project to suit, you might make the box larger for say computer discs or you might design a box to take coins or whatever.

2 When you have considered all the design and technique possibilities, take your carefully prepared and cut wood and build-up, glue and clamp a hollow rectangular tube.

3 Cap off the ends of the square-section tube with end-grain wood, make allowances for centre and cutting waste and then glue and clamp up.

4 Establish the line of the lid, cut the lid from the base, clean up the saw kerf and then screw the lid back to the base.

5 Now secure your prepared square section tube between centres, then with the tools of your choice turn off a cylinder.

6 Using callipers and a measure, check off the cylinder against the working drawings, and then take the wood to a good smooth and oiled finish.

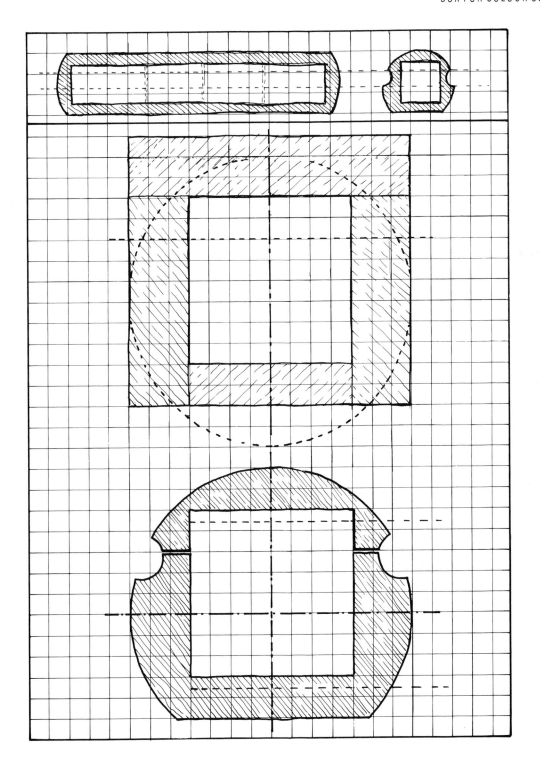

1 Working drawings. Top: the scale is 1 grid square to 1 in. Main: the scale is 4 grid squares to 1 in. See how the box shell has been built up around a 2×2 in cavity. The size of the box can be modified to suit.

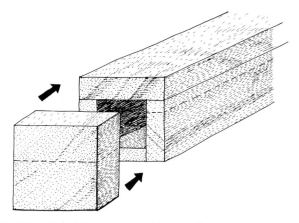

2 Build up the main box-tube form and then cap off the ends with end-grain wood. Note: if you are making the box for 2×2 in slides, build the box so that the cavity is about $2\frac{1}{8} \times 2\frac{1}{8}$ ins.

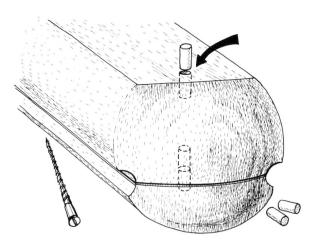

4 Route grooves along the separation between the lid and the base, fit and fix the brass hinges and finally plug the screw holes with matching or contrasting wood.

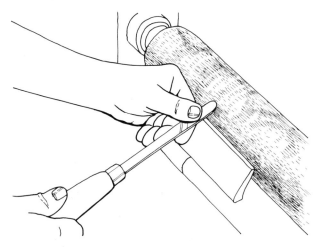

3 When the lid has been cut from the base, screw the base and lid together with long screws, then secure the wood between centres and turn off a well worked and finished dome-ended cylinder (see the working drawing).

7 With the box still secured between centres, or mounted on a special jig, cut routed grooves along the line of the lid/base kerf.

8 This done, remove the screws that hold the lid to the base, and then plug the holes with a contrasting wood to make a decorative feature.

9 Clean up the ends of the box and fit suitable interior partitions and brass hinge-and-catch furniture.

10 Finally check that all is well, then clean up the ends of the box, take the wood to a good finish and make good.

Afterthoughts and modifications

The initial box measurements are critical; when you are gluing up the box, make allowances for the thickness of the saw kerf.

The box ends are best built up from end grain wood. You might use a contrasting wood or wood of the same type and colour, as long as you allow at least $\frac{1}{2}$ in over length for centre-waste.

Rather than using screws to fix the lid to the base, you can use glue and paper (see the pencil box project).

With a project of this delicacy choose your wood with great care. Always check, prior to wood preparation, that the wood is free from splits, too many grain twists, stains and dead knots.

PEN SET HOLDER

Raymond William Hopper

Raymond's interest in woodturning started just after he left school when he bought himself an old metal spinning lathe. He made a selection of tools from worn files, old hacksaw blades and things like that, and then, for his first project, he turned wooden handles for the tools. He scraped away and cut a great many decorative rings and grooves, and then considered himself a proper woodturner. It was not long, however, before the whole house was knee-deep in dust and off-cuts, so the lathe just had to go.

Ray, now a carpenter and joiner, served his apprenticeship with a ladder and mobile tower manufacturer and then went on to work his way through various woodworking trades, from coffin making and shop fitting, to reproducing Queen Anne furniture. Now, many years later, he is the foreman in a joinery shop. Recently Raymond has been working on the firm's Jubilee Harrison Lathe, and this, together with a trip to a woodworking exhibition at Alexandra Palace, has again whetted his appetite for turning. At the exhibition he met Phil Jones, a woodturner who, as luck would have it, only lived a mile or two away. Phil, who gives tuition on a one-to-one basis, agreed to give him a series of lessons. These lessons altered Ray's whole approach to woodturning, so much so, that he went out and bought himself a Myford ML8 lathe, and converted part of a large greenhouse into a 64 sq ft workshop. There he can now make such delicate turned items as eggshell-thin goblets, bowls worked from green wood and dishes with natural bark rims.

Currently he sells his work at country craft fairs, or gives away turned items as much appreciated presents. When Ray first considered

this project, he wanted to get away from the round format, so he designed and turned an eccentric, two-centre base for a single pen, then, working through a series of prototypes, he eventually came up with the novel idea of have a double-plinth pen base worked on four centres. Selling his work at craft fairs and four centre turning, seems a far cry from Ray's school dust and debris days!

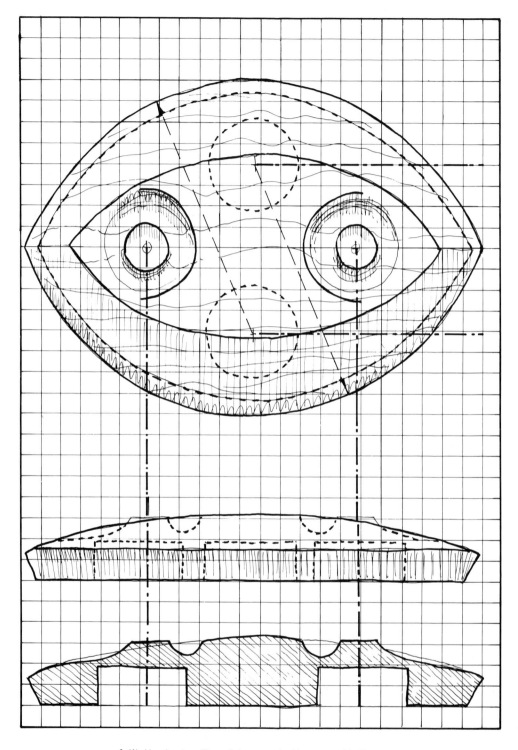

1 Working drawings. The scale is approx. 4 grid squares to 1 in. Note the four turning centres, see how two are used to turn off the petal profile, and two are used to work the pen positions. The whole form needs to be slightly undercut and well rubbed down.

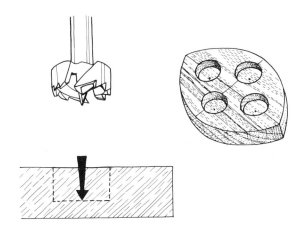

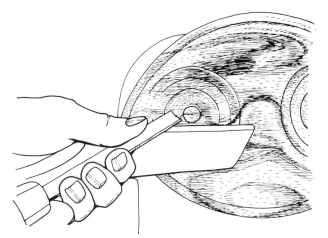

2 Establish the position of the four turning centres and then use a $1\frac{1}{8}$ in diameter saw tooth machine bit to bore out the $\frac{1}{2}$ in deep holes.

4 When you are working the pen-positions, aim to turn off nicely dished saucer forms, work with care and caution, and watch out for the off-centre swing of the wood.

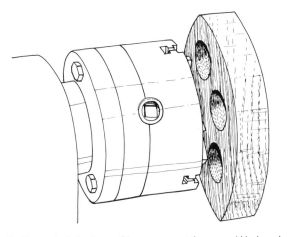

3 Working on the holes that are 2 ins apart, mount the prepared blank on the lathe, check that all is secure, and then turn off the petal profile. Note: as the wood is being turned off-centre, it is most important that the wood is well secured before the lathe is switched on.

TOOLS AND MATERIALS
roughing out gouge
spindle gouge
$1\frac{1}{8}$ in saw tooth drill bit
pens and fittings
all the usual workshop tools and materials
callipers
measure
sander filler
friction polish
canuba wax

WOOD
Small $6 \times 4 \times 1$ in English walnut off-cut. You can of course make this project from the wood of your choice.

Incidentally, Ray now buys his wood from a little-known sawmill where they convert local trees and sell walnut, elm and yew at very fair prices. This sawmill is hidden away in the woods, and Ray, is keeping its whereabouts to himself—wise man!

LATHE TYPE
A Myford ML8 with a $\frac{3}{4}$ HP motor and a three-jaw self centring chuck.

What to do
1 Have a look at the working drawings and the photographs. See how the piece of wood has been prepared and set out and note that there are four turning centres, two for the outside profile, and two for the dished and plateaued pen positions.

2 Once you have set the wood out and labelled it 'working face' and 'back', place it face down on the workbench, check the position of the four turning centres, and then drill four $\frac{1}{2}$ in deep holes with the $1\frac{1}{8}$ in saw tooth machine bit. Note: It is crucial that these four holes are at right angles to the working face of the wood.

3 Select one of the profile holes, that is one of the holes that are 2 ins apart, push the wood hard up against the closed jaws of the chuck, then gently turn the chuck key so that the chuck jaws expand inside the $1\frac{1}{8}$ in hole.

4 Check that the wood is secure and at right angles to the chuck face, then turn off half of the total pen holder profile. Repeat this turning procedure with the other profile hole.

5 Once you have achieved what you consider to be a good petal-lozenge profile and taken the wood to a reasonable finish, remount and secure the wood using one of the other holes.

6 Check that the wood is secure and at right angles, refresh your eye by having a look at the working drawings and the photograph, then very carefully turn off one of the little dished and plateaued pen positions. Repeat this procedure for the other pen position.

7 Once you have worked the wood from all four

centres, you can set about taking it to a good polished finish.

8 To remove and remount the workpiece only takes a few seconds so you can do the bulk of the polishing on the lathe.

9 Finally, take the wood from the lathe, drill the wood, mount the two pen holders, and the job is done.

Afterthoughts and modifications

With a four-centre project of this character, with the wood being worked off-centre and eccentrically, it is most important that the wood is secure. Watch out for judders, and be sure that your hands aren't clipped.

When you come to drilling the four $1\frac{1}{8}$ in diameter saw tooth bit holes, make sure that they are perfectly positioned and at right angles to the working face of the wood.

You might work this project on a screw chuck, an expanding chuck, a face plate, or whatever, as long as the wood is secure.

You might back the penholder with a piece of green felt.

OWL PLAQUE

John Huckvale

The satisfaction of creating something out of wood, the physical pleasure of handling natural materials—for John these are therapeutic experiences that help him to forget the trials and tribulations of daily commuting.

Working in an old coal cellar, complete with coal hole ventilation and coal dust, John started his woodworking ventures by whittling and carving. And it was from these small beginnings that he initially drew his woodturning inspiration. Having first carved a swordfish he mulled over the possibilities of making small decorative, sculptural shapes entirely on the lathe. One project led to another, a cat, a pig, and then a series of owl plaques. Very few of his pieces are designed in detail, usually he sees an idea in his mind's eye, starts working and then

as the form progresses, he makes sympathetic adaptations and modifications. John sees himself not as a professional woodturner, but as a hobbyist who enjoys the creative relaxation of turning.

LATHE TYPE
Myford ML8A, with a screw chuck.

TOOLS AND MATERIALS
scraper
parting tool
polyurethane varnish
PVA glue
callipers
paper
measure
pencils

WOOD TYPE
Prepared $\frac{1}{2}$ in thick dark oak off-cuts.

What to do

1 First take a good look at your chosen wood, check it over and make sure that it's free from loose knots, stains and splits.

2 Study the working drawings and then with pencil and sketch pad make your own design, form, and technique modifications.

3 With compass, ruler and a coping saw, set out the various circle blanks that go to make up the

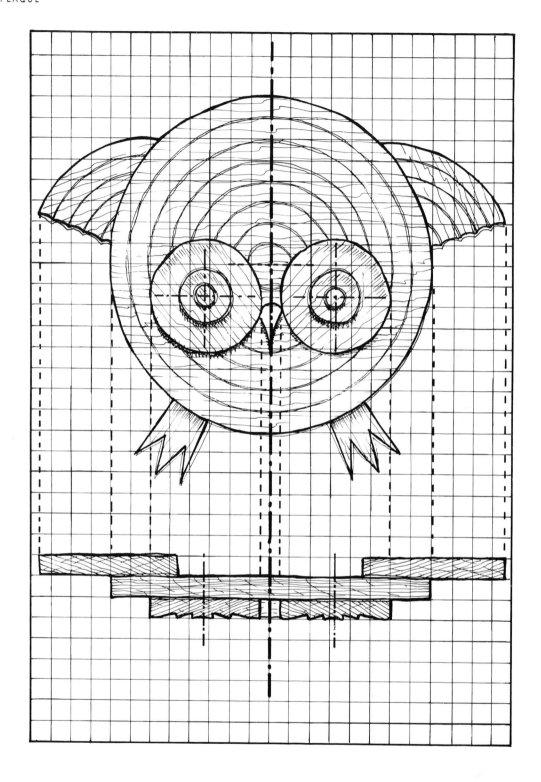

1 Working drawings. The scale is 1 grid square to $\frac{1}{4}$ inch. Note the direction of the wood grain and the multi-layered assembly of the various turnings.

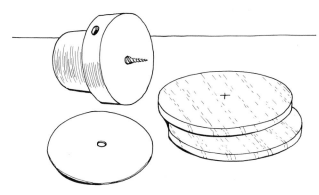

2 Locate the sawn blank on the chuck screw. If you have doubts about the screw to blank link-up, build out the wood thickness with a plywood-glue-and-paper waster, and use the full length of the screw.

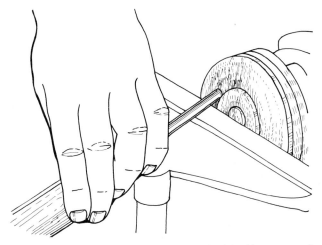

3 Work the eye discs with extra care. Dish the turning from side to centre, and slightly undercut the pupil to leave a plateau of proud wood.

project. You need a 4 in diameter circle for the body, two $1\frac{3}{8}$ in diameter circles for the eyes, one $2\frac{3}{4}$ in circle for the wings and various off-cuts for beak and feet.

4 Once the wood has been roughed out, take the body circle and locate it on the chuck screw.

5 Now with scraper and parting tool work a body disc that is about 4 ins in diameter, then use the parting tool to inscribe the seven or eight decorative concentric circles.

6 Locate one $1\frac{3}{8}$ in eye disc on the chuck and work a slightly dished form, undercut the pupil area so that it is left undercut and proud. Do this with both eye discs.

7 To make the wings, turn a $2\frac{3}{4}$ in diameter disc complete with decorative concentric circles, then quarter cut and whittle to make the two scalloped wing profiles.

8 With a coping saw work the beak and the feet from off-cuts.

9 Finally, once you have achieved all the turned and cut profiles, glue the beak and eyes to the front of the body, glue the wings and feet to the rear and then give the whole work a thin, well brushed, coat of polyurethane varnish.

Afterthoughts and modifications

John found that a few threads of the chuck screw provided a secure grip, however, it would be safer to glue a wood and paper waster disc onto the back of the work and then use the full length of the screw.

Removing the waster discs might be a bit of a problem. If this is the case, they could be left in place and sandwich-mounted to give an added dimension. If the eyes were set out from the body by the thickness of the wasters, the total sculpture would perhaps be more dynamic and exciting.

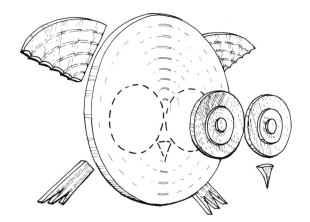

4 When you have achieved all the turnings, cut, carve and adjust as you think fit. Then use PVA glue to fix the eyes and beak to the front of the body, and the wings and feet to the rear.

SECRET TRINKET BOX

Norman James Law

Norman has been woodturning for about two years. He admits it has become an obsession! Although he enjoys the whole turning process, the part that gives him the most satisfaction, is the 'finish'. The shine of the grain, the crisp, considered lines of the turned forms, these aspects of the craft give Norman immense pleasure. And of course, there is the social side of the craft, friends and relations taking an interest and meeting new people at craft fairs.

Norman is prepared to spend many long hours making prototypes. For example, with this particular project, he made five pre-competition boxes, three in Brazilian walnut, one in yew and yet another in mahogany. His total involvement and eye for detail are obviously paying off: 'a bowl I made recently, a

very ornamental bowl, has sold for a £100 ... made from a yew root, it is, I must admit, my pride and joy'.

As for his lathe, Norman's first machine was a 1932 converted metal lathe, but he now works on a Harrison Union Graduate.

LATHE TYPE
A Harrison Union Graduate with a selection of chuck types.

TOOLS AND MATERIALS
2 in roughing out gouge
$\frac{1}{4}$ in gouge
$\frac{1}{4}$ in beading tool
$\frac{1}{2}$ in skew chisel
fluted parting tool
callipers
pencil and measure
workout paper
cellulose sanding sealer
French polish
and of course all the other run of the mill tools and materials

WOOD
Several small lime off-cuts, or a single cylindrical blank.

What to do
1 Have a good look at the working drawings, note the complexities of the project and then set out your wood and tools.

2 Secure the wood in the chuck and then, with tools of your choice, turn off the top and side profiles of the main cylinder.

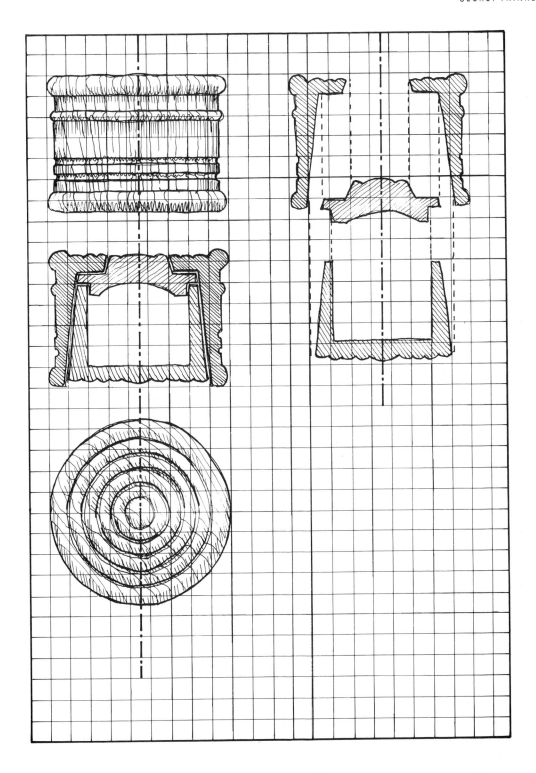

1 Working drawings. The scale is 3 grid squares to 1 in. See how the three turnings come together to make a classic pillbox form and note that for a successful project, the inside box needs to be a perfect, tight friction-fit.

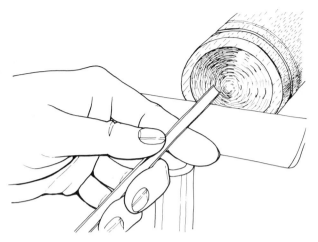

2 Secure the protected cylinder in the jaws of the chuck and then turn out a nicely tapered hollow form.

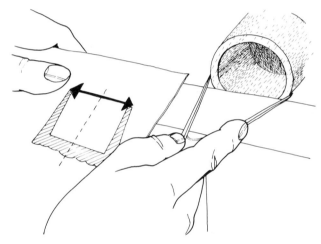

3 Using a template and callipers, work and taper the inner box until it is a good friction-fit.

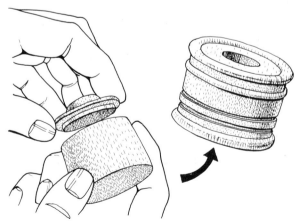

4 Prior to turning the beads, put the box back together. Try to achieve a totally considered form.

3 Don't at this stage cut the beads on the top of the box. Instead, work a hole that starts at a diameter of about $1\frac{1}{8}$ in and tapers into the wood to a depth of about $\frac{1}{4}$ in.

4 When you have achieved a well considered form and worked the tapered lid-hole, part off and remove the remains of the blank from the chuck.

5 Take the solid turned form, cover it with a protective strapping (Norman uses inner-tube rubber) and reverse and secure the wood so that the hole end is in the chuck.

6 When the solid form has been well mounted, cut into the wood and work the tapered interior, be careful not to overtighten the chuck.

7 Now, in the same way, turn off the inner box and the lid. Aim to work an inner form that is a perfect, tapered friction-fit.

8 When you have achieved a good outer shell, a inner box, put the project together, mount it in the lathe and turn off the lid and base rings.

9 Finally, sand and trim to a good fit, rub down, and then take the wood to a good finish.

Afterthoughts and modifications

This project is deceptively simple. Be warned— if the inner and outer forms are too tight you might split the wood, but if they are too loose the project will fail, so the tapering needs to be worked with great care and caution.

Norman recommends a working speed of about 2250 RPM.

Instead of protecting the solid form with rubber strapping and securing it in a standard chuck, you might consider using an expanding collet chuck, or a special.

Before you work this project, turn off a prototype and establish the angle of taper and the order of working.

Before you start turning, always check your wood for possible problems and bring your tools to good order.

SET OF THIMBLES

Ernest Ronald Lloyd

Ernest Ronald Lloyd, his friends call him Ron, is a farmworker and as a result has a particularly close affinity with the countryside around him and the various changes nature can have upon the land. From the soil, wildlife and woodlands to the little pieces of wood that he chooses to work on his lathe, Ron appreciates and loves them all in different ways. He bought his first set of woodturning tools, a standard gouge, a skew chisel and a parting tool over 30 years ago and they still serve him well. He then went on to build his own lathe out of wood.

Perhaps Ron's enthusiasm for the craft dwindled a little when he got married and started a family, but now, many years later, his interest has been rekindled. He has purchased a 'proper' lathe of which he is very proud and now he is working again with his aromatic favourites — yew, oak, beech and elm. Ron considers himself to be a self-taught amateur who is always seeking perfection in his work. He is not a great one for intricate plans or drawings, instead he sees a germ of an idea in his mind's eye and then, with characteristic Welsh compulsiveness, goes straight out into his modest old granary workshop and starts coaxing the wood into shape. As to why Ron likes woodturning — it's simple enough, it gives him pleasure, and he derives great satisfaction from being able to say 'I made that'.

LATHE TYPE
An Arundel K450 with a $\frac{1}{2}$ HP motor and a selection of chucks.

TOOLS AND MATERIALS
1 in standard roughing gouge

1 in skew chisel
$\frac{1}{2}$ in hollow gouge
round end scraper (Ron uses an old $\frac{1}{4}$ in mortise chisel ground to a finger nail profile)
callipers
pencil
measure
2 in nail cut, ground and mounted in a pedestal drill and used in the manner of a drop forge
bradawl
compass
workout card and paper
wax polish (or polyurethane varnish)
glasspaper
letter transfers
wax
small piece of red silk
small disc of foam
various drill bits
and of course other more general workshop tools and materials

WOODS
A short length of yew bough for the lid and base as end grain only appears on each end. (It is important to work down the grain as yew can 'pick up'.) Various off-cuts for the small thimbles.

What to do
1 Have a look at the working drawings and the photograph on page 23 and see how the project consists of five small thimbles all set and mounted on a lid-covered presentation base. Note the silk lined large thimble and how each of the small thimbles is made from a different

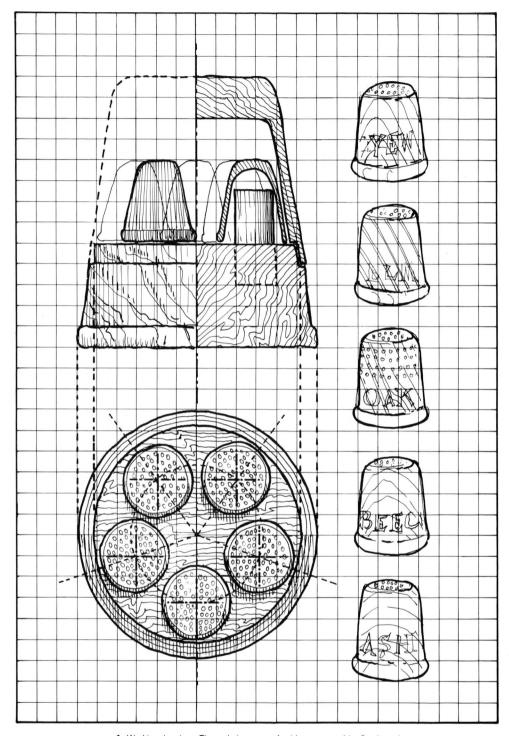

1 Working drawings. The scale is approx. 4 grid squares to 1 in. See how the base is divided into five parts, and how the five little thimbles each sit on a dowel spigot. The placing of the thimbles, the angle at which the sides of the little thimbles are cut and the interior profile of the large thimble, all need to be well considered at the design stage.

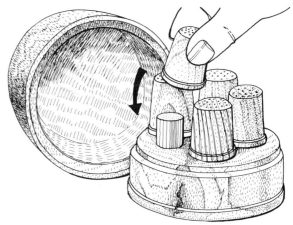

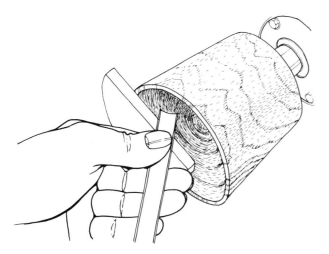

2 When you have worked the outside profile of the large thimble, check with your working drawings, and then turn off the inside of the lid.

4 When you have set the base out, drilled the five dowel holes, placed the five thimbles, and generally taken the whole project to a good fit and finish, then you can rub down, apply the name transfers and varnish.

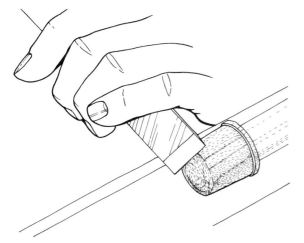

3 Piece at a time, locate the little thimbles on a chuck spigot, check that all is secure and then turn off the characteristic profile. When you have achieved your first thimble, cut and work all the others so that they are identical.

named wood. Consider the total character of the project, then draw up your own design modifications to suit.

2 When you have assessed the project and all its design and technique implications, set out your prepared wood and check it for faults. Reject any wood that looks less than perfect.

3 Take the piece of yew, mount it on the small face plate, check that all is secure and then start work.

4 Turn a total lid-and-base form, cut a rebate

for the lid/base line, take a series of calliper readings just to make sure that all is well, and then part off.

5 Now, with the lid still attached to the face plate, cut, work and hollow its interior, check that the inside rim rebate is a good fit, and then part off.

6 Mount the base in a wooden chuck and then clean up the parted face.

7 Have a look at the working drawings, then turn off five small dowels, drill the base and tap them home.

8 Turn and turn about, work the small thimbles on the screw chuck, clean out their interiors and then part them off.

9 Using a face plate and a wooden chuck (or a special chuck of your choice), take a small thimble, mount it on a chuck-spigot and then take its top to a well considered domed finish. Do this with all five small thimbles.

10 Make a stencil template for the top of the large thimble and then drill, punch, or otherwise set out, the characteristic thimble dents.

11 Cut and work the silk lining, reverse, position and glue the lining around the inside rim of the lid, and then turn it in on itself so as to cover the glue-fixing.

12 Cover a foam disc with silk and carefully place and glue-fix it into the thimble lid so as to cover the cut edge of the lining.

13 Punch-mark the small thimbles, then check and finish.

14 Finally, rub all the work down and apply several coats of wax polish, rubbing down between coats. Apply the name transfers, sit the thimbles on the pegs, checking that all is well, and the job is done.

Afterthoughts and modifications

If you do decide to use a pedestal drill to drop-dent the large thimble, be careful that you don't split the wood.

Leave the walls of the small thimbles fairly thick.

When you have turned the base and the lid interior, fit them together and turn the outside lid profile so that it runs smoothly into the base.

Lining the thimble lid is rather tricky, sticky and finger twisting—you might modify the project at this point and leave the lid unlined.

It might be as well to make a prototype.

FRUIT BOWL ON PILLARS

Arthur McVittie

Arthur enjoys woodturning because of the pleasures and rewards of being able to control the tools and the materials. He feels fulfilled and totally relaxed when, during the creative process, his imagination and skill work together to produce a co-ordinated whole. Arthur served his apprenticeship as a cart-wright and wheelwright, probably one of the last, as sadly, with the coming of the tractor and mass-production, the trade more or less died overnight. He eventually became a self-employed supervisor on building and civil engineering works. Lately ill health has forced Arthur to stop work and stay at home, but undaunted, he has returned to the workbench.

In his garage workshop, Arthur has had time to mull over his working career. He remembers as an apprentice making wheel hubs, he remembers working on a steam driven wood-bed lathe and with these times remembered Arthur has realized that he should never have left the bench. Now 30 years later, Arthur has gone back to his first love, he has bought his own lathe and has decided that woodturning is going to be part of his future. If you are looking for a craftsman to restore your wagon or farm cart, then Arthur is your man and he can be contacted through the editors. He is now busy rebuilding the wooden wheel rims for an ancient 'boneshaker' bicycle—not full time you understand, at the moment it's just a hobby. A craftsman, a man with unique skills, a man with a new future—Arthur is all of these.

LATHE TYPE
An Apollo Woodstyler with 48 ins between centres, a $\frac{3}{4}$ HP motor, 12 in diameter over bed and 17 ins outboard.

TOOLS AND MATERIALS
$\frac{3}{8}$ in deep fluted bowl gouge
$\frac{1}{8}$ in parting tool
1 in square ended scraper
$\frac{1}{4}$ in spindle gouge
bevel ended scraper (Arthur made his from an old wood chisel)
glue
Craft Lac
Bri Wax
hand drill and $\frac{3}{8}$ in bit
callipers
compass
workout paper
and all the other usual workshop bits and pieces

WOODS
A slab of $2\frac{1}{2}$ in thick oak for the bowl, a 1 in thick slab of oak for the base, a piece of $\frac{1}{2}$ in thick oak for the foot ring and small off-cuts of lime for the pillars.

What to do

1 Study the working drawings and the photograph on page 9 and see how the project is made up in four parts—the bowl, the base, the foot ring and the eight pillars. Note how the base has been dished and hollowed on both sides.

2 Check your wood for possible faults and blemishes.

3 Screw the $2\frac{1}{2}$ in thick slab of oak to the face plate, check that it is secure, then arrange your tools so that they are comfortably to hand.

4 With the tools of your choice, cut and hollow the inside and outside profiles of the bowl, aim

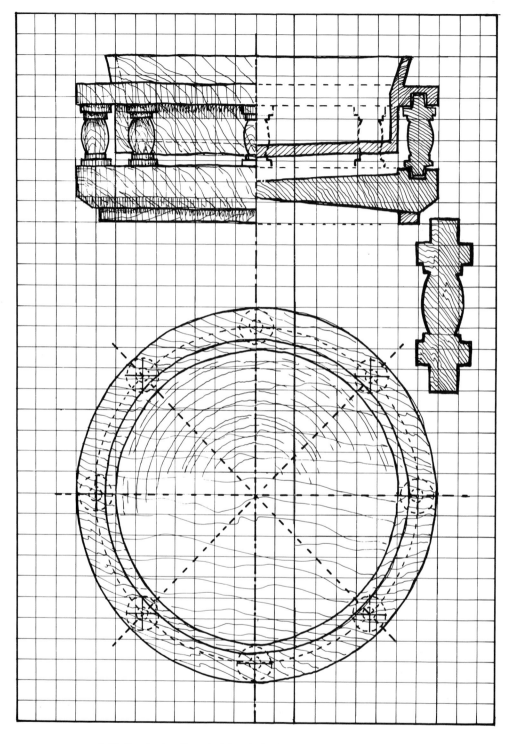

1 Working drawings. The scale of the main drawing is approx. 2 grid squares to
1 in. The scale of the pillar/spindle section is 4 grid squares to 1 in. See how the
composite project is made up from eleven separate turnings, the bowl, the base,
the base ring, and eight spindles or pillars.

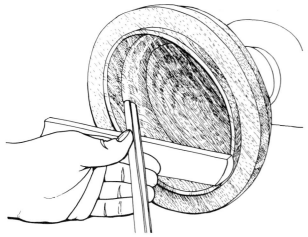

2 Screw the main blank onto a face plate, check that the wood is secure and then turn off the dished and flanged form, take the wood to a good finish.

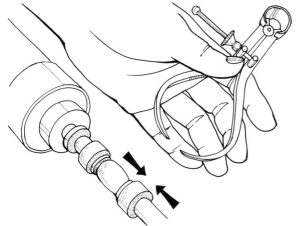

3 Turn the eight lime spindles between centres, use callipers and a cardboard template to achieve eight identical spigot-ended pillars.

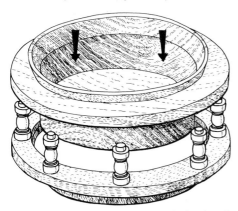

4 To assemble the composite form, glue and place the foot ring, glue the eight spindles and place them in the base holes and glue and locate the spindle spigots in the bowl flange holes. Finally, check that the alignment of bowl and spindles to the base is correct, then place the work carefully between boards and clamp up.

to establish the good clean, sharp angled cuts that characterize this project.

5 Cut and work the underside of the balustrade, check that it is wide enough to take the pillars, and then continue to turn off the bowl base.

6 Remove the bowl, mount the wood for the base and then set about turning off the balustrade edge profile and slightly dished interior.

7 Reverse the wood on the chuck and then turn the base until it is concave in section.

8 Remove the base, mount the $\frac{1}{2}$ in thick piece of wood, check on the placing of the chuck screws and then turn off a square section foot hoop.

9 This done set about turning off the eight identical lime wood spindles or pillars, work the wood between centres and check your work against a series of calliper readings, or with a cardboard template.

10 When you have achieved all the various parts that make up the project, and have taken them to a good finish, clear the worksurface of all clutter and then set out the parts on the workbench.

11 With a measure and a compass, mark out the position of the eight pillars.

12 Drill and work the sixteen $\frac{3}{8}$ in holes, eight on the underside of the bowl balustrade, and eight on the topside of the base rim.

13 Fit, place and glue the eight pillars, position the base foot and then clamp up.

14 Finally, rub down with a scrap of fine glasspaper and then bring whole project to a good waxed finish.

Afterthoughts and modifications
You might work the bowl and foot from a single $1\frac{1}{2}$ in thick slab of wood.

Establishing the position of the eight pillars is a bit tricky. If you have problems, make and use a cardboard template.

PIN CUSHION

Albert Thomas Parsler

Albert, usually known as Alb, first started woodturning when he was sent off to boarding school in 1946 at the tender age of 11. A couple of years later he was streamed and placed on a trade training course, and so it was, lucky lad, that he spent most of his formative years in a carpentry shop. By the time he was 15, he was busy producing all manner of first-rate turned and cabinet–built items, most of which were sold for school funds. In this way Albert had a thorough grounding in carpentry and was ready to face the world. On leaving school he was employed by an antique restoration firm. Alb's interest in woodturning has persisted and strengthened over the years, and at last, he has found the time to pursue this interest.

For many years he has been concerned about timber wastage having watched bits of old furniture being burnt and demolition timber being thrown out. In response to this concern, he has tried to rescue, recycle and give new life to really beautiful and sometimes irreplacable wood, so it might not be lost. Alb's brick and timber workshop is about 12×12 ft and into this relatively large area he has set out a new Arundel K450 lathe, a bandsaw and his various Wolf, Marples and Sorby tools. For this project he rescued and used a piece of mahogany from an old bookcase. As to why he makes pin cushions, Alb thinks that they are great fun to turn and work and they make a nice gift 'for the lady who has everything'. Better still, they are an eye-catching feature when he sets them out on his yearly craft stall.

LATHE TYPE

An Arundel K450 with a $\frac{1}{2}$ HP motor and a variety of chucks, a face plate and an expanding chuck.

TOOLS AND MATERIALS

selection of standard turning gouges and scrapers
workout paper
compass
piece of fabric for covering the cushion
piece of 2 in thick foam
length of decorative braid to match the cover fabric
small quantity of gimp pins
Copydex or another suitable fabric/wood glue
you will also need
measure
template card
hammer
scissors

WOODS

A 1 in thick, 7 in diameter hardwood blank, a $\frac{1}{2}$ in thick, 5 in diameter blank for the tacking disc and a short length of square section 1×1 in timber.

What to do

1 Have a look at the working drawings and photograph on page 12 and note how Alb draws his design inspiration from Victorian furniture forms. See also how the pin cushion has four feet, a finished diameter of 6 ins, and a foot-to-pad height of about 3 ins.

2 Screw the 7 in diameter blank to the face plate, check that all is secure, and then mount the wood on the lathe.

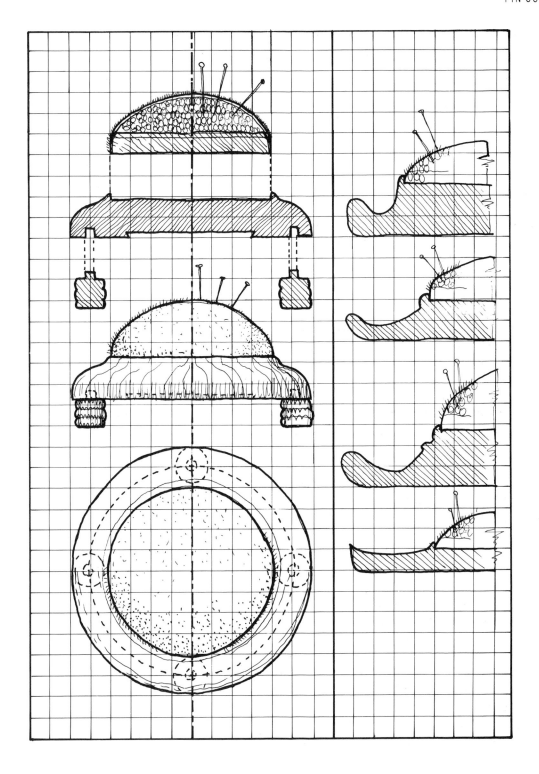

1 Working drawings. Left: the scale is 2 grid squares to 1 in. Right: not to scale.
See how the pin cushion is put together, note the peg feet and the upholstered
and padded cushion.

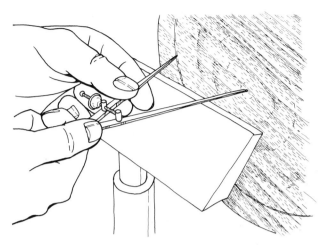

2 Screw the base blank on the face plate and mark off the position of the various cuts with a compass or callipers.

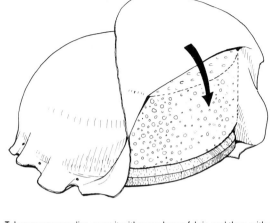

4 Take your sponge disc, cover it with your chosen fabric, and then, with great care, stretch the fabric over the tacking disc edges and fix with gimp pins.

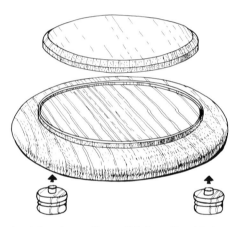

3 Cut and work the various profiles, establish the position of the feet, and cut a loose fitting tacking disc.

3 With the tools of your choice, turn the face of the blank to a smooth true finish, and then turn an undercut recess to take the collet of your expanding chuck

4 Take the wood off the face plate, secure the collet of the expanding chuck in the undercut recess, and then mount the whole works on the lathe.

5 Check that all is secure, take a few calliper readings from the master design, or cut a card-board template, and then proceed to cut the various curves that make up the cushion base.

6 Cut and work a $4\frac{1}{2}$ in diameter flat-face recess, tidy up the rim and lip, and then take the whole turning to a smooth, sanded, sealed and polished finish.

7 Mount the 5 in blank on the face plate, and turn it off until its diameter is slightly less than $4\frac{1}{2}$ ins, see the working drawings.

8 When you have achieved a good base, and a loose-fitting tacking blank, mount the 1×1 in square wood between centres, and turn off four $\frac{3}{4}$ in diameter, spigotted feet. Give the four feet identical decorative rings and grooves, cut the foot profiles to suit your overall design theme.

9 Measure and set out the base, and then drill, glue and fix the four foot-knobs.

10 Now clear up all your bench clutter, make sure the worksurface is perfectly clean, and then set out your tools and material.

11 Place the 2 in thick disc of foam on the tacking blank, position your chosen cover fabric, and then, with great care, pin the fabric to the blank edges.

12 Carefully ease the fabric and the foam over

the chamfered edge of the tacking blank, make sure all the bulky tucks and folds have been eased out, and then fix with gimp pins.

13 Place the cushion in the base recess, check that all is correct and as described, and then fix from the underside of the base with a single brass screw.

14 Finally cut the decorative braid to size, and mount it round the cushion with a small amount of Copydex glue.

Afterthoughts and modifications

On an uneven surface three feet give better stability than four.

When you are choosing the cover fabric, choose a fine weave. If the fabric frays easily, fix the cut edge with glue or a zig-zag machine stitch.

When you are fixing the decorative braid, be very careful not to mark the fabric with the glue. If in doubt, you might secure the braid with a fine thread and an upholsterer's needle rather than use glue.

The cushion rim—that is, the rim that goes round the cushion recess is rather fragile. When you turn this area, work with extra care.

COTTON NESTS

Leonard Barrington Piers

A senior systems consultant in the Hi-Tech electronics industry, and later a heart attack victim, Len decided in 1985 to ease the stress of everyday living by trying his hand at woodturning. A creative person by nature, he needed to express this creativity. Certainly his occupation provides an outlet for this need, but it lacks the personal and practical touch.

Woodturning, he soon discovered, was the answer. For him it has become an expressive, design-related medium through which he can explore colour, form and texture.

Len has no problem in finding inspiration for his projects, the woodturning ideas come tumbling out in a never ending stream, limited only by the time available. Of course his wife Jill could have sat back and watched, but that's not her style. She is now a first class turner's mate and fast becoming a woodturner in her own right. The extension on their house is a workshop containing benching, the lathe, a grinder and other more general facilities. Their woodturning activities have also overflowed into the adjoining garage, which now contains a bandsaw and a sizable stock of timber.

As you might have guessed, since Len is a design consultant, when he starts a project, he follows through his initial ideas by making all manner of prototypes, conducting mini surveys and generally drawing up new designs, working in design changes and so on.

LATHE TYPE
ELU DB180 lathe with various face plates and chucks.

TOOLS AND MATERIALS
A good range of tools facilitates this project but Len used mostly a long and strong bowl gouge. You will also need:
short length of $\frac{3}{8}$ in diameter thread rod
nut to fit the rod
resin glue
hand drill
two drill bits, $\frac{1}{2}$ in and $\frac{3}{4}$ in or a Jacob's chuck
callipers
workout paper
pencil
measure
wire wool
garnet paper
sanding sealer
wax
the use of an expanding collet chuck or self centring $\frac{3}{4}$ in jaw chuck
and all the usual workshop tools and materials

WOOD
This project is made in Ash, choose well-seasoned off-cuts to suit.

What to do

1 Have a look at the working drawings and the photograph on page 21 and see how the three nests or bowls are each designed to hold seven standard size cotton reels. See also how the cotton reels are contained within the nests, and how the nests slide on the central rod.

2 When you have studied the project, modified the design and generally come to grips with the working details, mark out your wood and set out

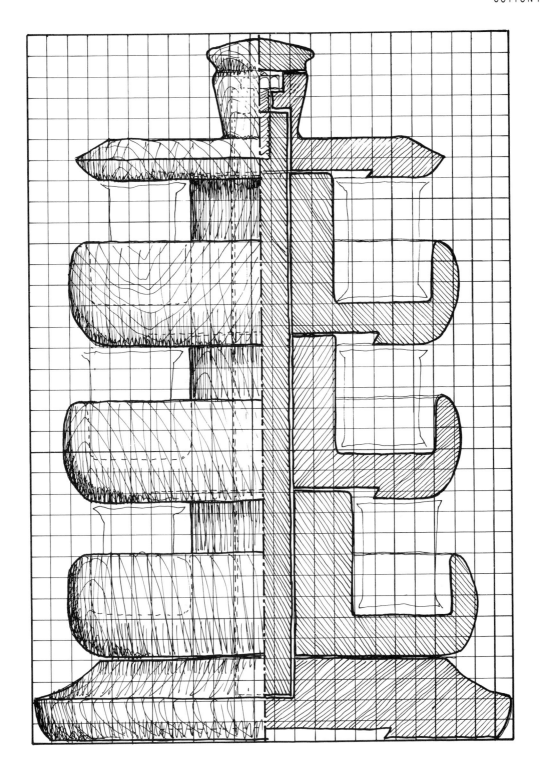

1 Working drawings. The scale is 4 grid squares to 1 in. See how the dishes or trays slide on a central column and how, when the lid is screwed in place, the cotton reels are contained and yet at the same time on display.

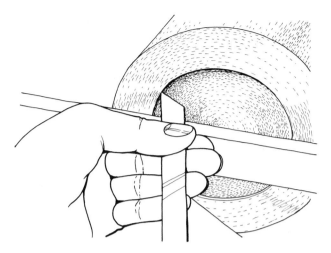

2 Work the underside of all the blanks and cut an expanding collet recess.

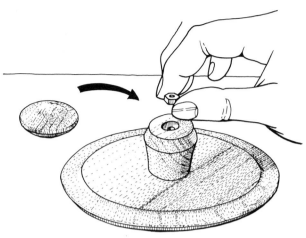

4 When you have cut and worked the lid cavity, fit and glue the nut, check that everything is well aligned, then place and glue the lid cap and trim to a good finish.

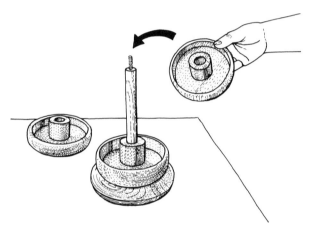

3 Bore a hole through each of the nest bowls so that they are an easy fit on the central column.

your working area. Rough blanks need to be sawn for turning.

3 Screw the base blank to a face plate, mount it on the lathe, then turn off the base and a recess for expanding or alternative chucks.

4 Once you have worked the underside of the base blank, and have established the size of the recess, repeat the procedure with the three nest blanks and the lid.

5 Now, using an expanding collet chuck, mount the blanks in turn, and cut the three bowls, the base and the lid.

6 Although the three nest bowls are identical in design and the turning technique relatively simple, when you come to turning the vertical walls you will need to work with care and caution.

7 When you have achieved what you consider to be a good lidded form, turn off and part the upper section of the knob, and drill a suitable size nut cavity (see working drawing).

8 Now drill a $\frac{3}{8}$ in hole through the lid and pierce the nut cavity.

9 Take the $\frac{3}{4}$ in drill and work a blind hole in the base, a hole right through each of the nest bowls and a 1 in deep hole in the underside of the lid (see the working drawing).

10 When all the forms have been turned, worked and finished, clear the work surface of all clutter and dust, and then set out the wood glue and the resin glue, the nut and the short length of threaded rod.

11 First, using the resin glue, fix the rod into the top of the dowel, and fix the nut inside the lid cavity. Check that the rod and the nut are well aligned and the thread clear of glue. Leave it to set.

12 Finally, place and glue the top section of the lid-knob, aligning the grain and glue the central column dowel in the base, check on alignment, and the job is done.

Afterthoughts and modifications

Note: With the use of a Jacob's chuck in tailstock (available in ELU DB180) stages 7 and 8 can be reduced to a simple drill change and stage 9 could have been carried out at stage 5.

At the design stage, it might be as well to visit a suitable museum with collections of 18th- and 19th-century sewing room paraphernalia.

The project might be re-designed so that there are more or less than three nests, or so that the top nest is a lidded button box.

Rather than using a metal rod and nut, you might use a suitable wood-cutting tap and die to thread the top of the central dowel and the inside of the lid.

The project might also be modified so that it is possible to store a certain number of non-standard cotton reels, or you might consider using cotton reel location dowels.

CHECKERED EDGE FRUIT BOWL

Dr Peter Ramsden
(who also designed the next item)

'It all started when I wanted wheels for the toys that I was making for my children'. And so it was that Peter first took up wood turning. At that time he was using a Black and Decker mini 'lathe' powered by an electric drill, which did him good service even when, as one of his first projects, he made a chess set. And so one project led to another. Now Peter has turned one end of his garage into a well equipped workshop complete with a Myford ML8 ¾ HP 4 speed lathe, a small band saw, a hand held circular saw, an electric chain saw, an old treadle lathe fitted with a large tool-sharpening carborundum, a Sjoborg bench, and another heavy bench made up from reclaimed timber.

Peter has always liked wood, and particularly the look and feel of turned objects. Woodturn-ing is clean, if dusty, and as a doctor in general practice this is important. As for designs and ideas, he looks to *Practical Woodworking* magazine, various library picture books, and, perhaps his most inspirational source, a book on antique treen. First he takes basic measurements, then he scales to size and adjusts to suit. A man of many interests, squash, golf, photography and collecting antique medical instruments, Peter turns these articles as presents or for special commissions. But as with these original and rather tricky projects, he simply likes to 'see if it can be done'.

LATHE TYPE
Myford ML8 ¾ HP, 550 watts, four speed lathe with in and outboard turning.

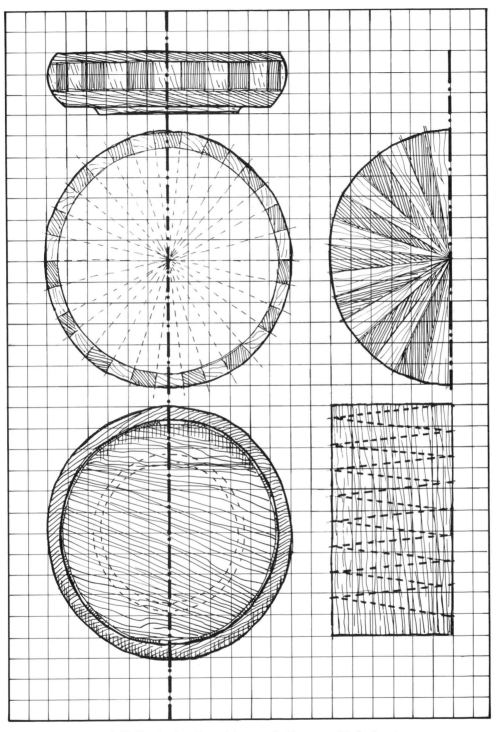

1 Working drawings. The scale is approx. 3 grid squares to 1 in. See how the rim disc has been cut from the bowl foot, and also how the checkered layer is made of thirty contrasting cake-wedge slices. Note: the drawing detail that shows how the wedges might be cut from a single piece of wood is only diagrammatic.

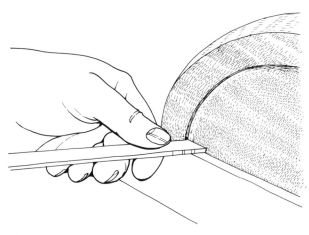

2 Establish the size of the bowl, then turn off the foot and remove the rim hoop.

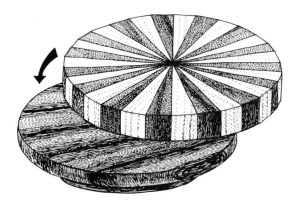

3 Cut, work and glue the checkered cake-wedge slices to the upper face of the foot-worked blank.

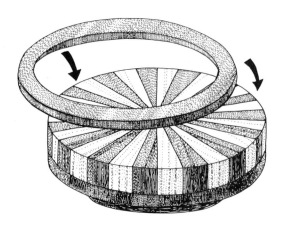

4 Glue and clamp the rim hoop in position, let the glue dry, and then turn off a bowl form.

TOOLS AND MATERIALS

set of 6 Marples small tools
2 Henry Taylor tools
long turning gouge
$\frac{1}{4}$ in gouge
parting tool and various other large tools
faceplate
wood glue
sanding sealer
wire wool
beeswax
solid polish
all the usual workshop tools like
pencils
compass
workout paper
measure

WOODS

A piece of mahogany about $10 \times 10 \times 2$ ins, another piece of mahogany about $9 \times 7 \times 2$ ins and a piece of sycamore $9 \times 7 \times 2$ ins. Note: you might use any contrasting light and dark woods.

What to do

1 First check your wood over, then have a look at the photograph and the working drawings and see how the bowl has been built up, cake-like, with a mahogany base, a checkered cake-wedge infill and a mahogany rim.

2 Note how the rim of the bowl has been economically built-up from a hoop cut from around the bowl foot, then mark out the pre-pared wood accordingly.

3 Screw the $10 \times 10 \times 2$ ins slab of mahogany to the face plate, and turn a blank that is about $9\frac{1}{2}$ ins in diameter.

4 Now with the tools of your choice, establish the size of the bowl foot, then cut-in and remove the rim hoop.

5 Work the foot ring profile then remove the wood from the faceplate.

6 Note the size and angle of the 30 contrasting cake-wedge slices that go to make up the check-

ered infill. Then cut, work, glue and clamp the infill on the upper face of the foot-worked blank.

7 When the glue is dry, screw the face plate to the bowl foot, then true and turn the glued face to size.

8 Glue, place and clamp the rim hoop on top of the partially worked bowl blank.

9 When the glue is dry, turn off the outside profile, work the interior hollow, and shape the rim.

10 Finally, seal, sand, rub down, clear up the bench waste, and then take the bowl to a good finish with wood swarf, and beeswax polish.

Afterthoughts and modifications
Cutting a rim hoop from the bowl foot is rather tricky. You could change the project slightly by building and clamping a straightforward three layer blank.

There are thirty slices in all, 15 sycamore and

15 mahogany, note the 12° angle of cut.

When you are choosing two different wood types, make sure they have similar working characteristics.

Peter used an alternative technique which achieves the same effect but requires less wood. Instead of the cake-wedge method, make the checkered edge by using pieces of sycamore and mahogany measuring $20 \times 1 \times 1$ ins. Plane these pieces of wood at an angle of 6° on either side of the squared up timber to make a stubby wedge and then cut this into fifteen 1 in sections. Glue these sections alternately to build up the ring, making sure that they are pressed down hard onto a flat surface and a band of wire must be tightened around them while they set. When completed, glue and clamp to the bowl foot and once dry the whole thing can be put on the lathe to true up the surface. Note: this technique requires extreme care when planing the mahogany and sycamore into the wedge and again when cutting into sections.

POMANDER

Dr Peter Ramsden

LATHE TYPE
A Myford ML 8 with an expanding chuck.

TOOLS AND MATERIALS
set of 6 small Marples tools
selection of scrapers
woodcarvers spoon bit gouge (or similar)
drill chuck
expanding or special chuck
suitable saw tooth drill bit
and of course you will also need such workshop items as
pencils
callipers
wire wool
sanding sealer
wax polish

WOOD
2 pieces of lime about $3 \times 3 \times 3$ ins.

What to do
1 Have a good look at the working drawings and photographs, then with pencil, measure and compass, set out your wood accordingly.

2 Using a special chuck, either one with an expanding collet or face plate rings, secure the wood, a block at a time, and turn off the inside of both the pomander base and the lid, and the outside base profile.

3 Work and establish the rim and lip on both the base and the lid, aim for a good tight fit.

4 Now with measure, compass and the small

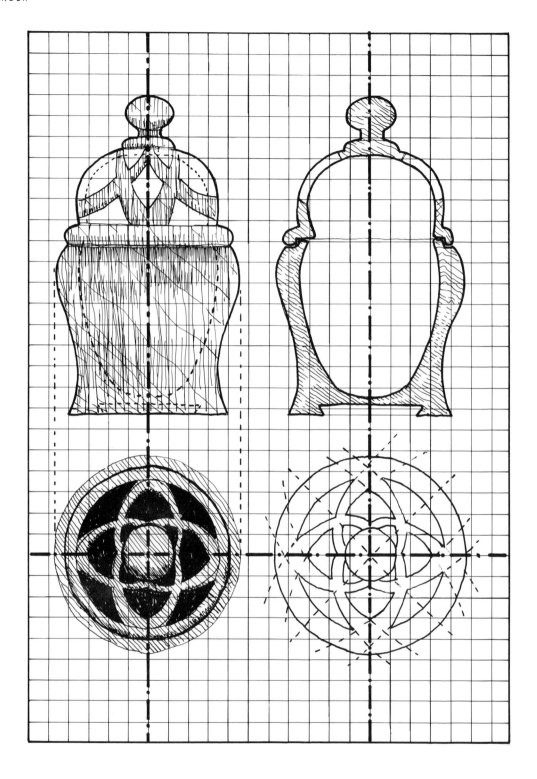

1 Working drawings. The scale is 4 grid squares to 1 in. Use a compass or a paper template to establish the pierced lid design.

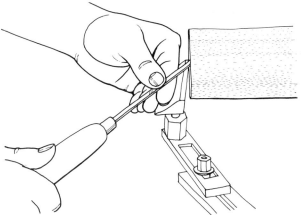

2 Mount the wood on the lathe and then, a piece at a time, turn off the inside profile of both the base and the lid.

spoon bit gouge, set-out, mark and carve the inside of the lid.

5 Aim to achieve an inside-lid carved depth of about $\frac{1}{4}$ to $\frac{1}{2}$ in. Don't force the tool into the grain of the lime, just work with delicate scooping cuts.

6 When the inside-lid has been carved, set the base on the lathe, fit the lid to the base, and then stop for a while and consider the desired profile.

7 When all is secure, turn the outside of the pomander lid down as far as you dare, work until the struts or lattice of the design can be seen.

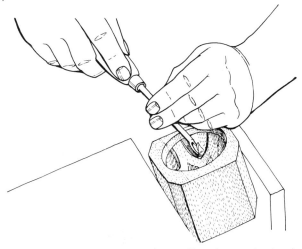

3 Once you have established the inside-lid profile, and set out the pierced design, cut away the waste 'windows' to a depth of about $\frac{1}{4}$ to $\frac{1}{2}$ in.

8 When the various 'windows' of the lattice have been pierced, take the lid off the base, and clean it up with a fine-point, keen edged tool.

9 Finally put the lid on the base, then sand, seal and polish to a good finish.

Afterthoughts and modifications

This project could be worked with a screw chuck and a small face plate. It doesn't matter, as long as the general order of working is followed.

When you have turned the outside of the lid down as far as the pierced lattice, then work with extra care, and only remove the finest whisps of wood.

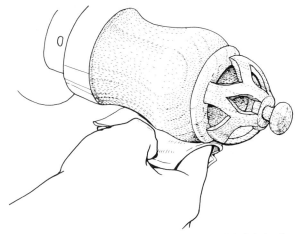

4 Mount the base-and-lid on the lathe, turn off the lid until the 'windows' are nicely established, then take the whole project to a wax polished finish.

EGG STAND

Eric William Rumbles

For Eric, woodturning is a totally refreshing and tranquil hobby, he likes nothing better than to go out to his garage workshop and to make something on the lathe—Eric enjoys every moment carefully preparing the wood, roughing-out blanks, taking the wood to a good finish, polishing and waxing, and in this way creating an item that not only looks good, but is also lovely to feel and hold. To sit down in his workshop surrounded by his equipment, the lathe, bandsaw, pillar drill, router, sander and, of course, the usual planes and chisels, and to scribble out ideas, draw up working details, and then to work the spinning wood, as far as Eric is concerned, these are all slippered pleasures.

When it comes to designing and making, his training and background stand him in good stead. He spent 31 years working with Vickers Engineering, and then 15 years with the Welcome Foundation as an engineering estimator. Eric is a craftsman of the old school. When he sat down to design this particular project, he wanted to do a turning that required the production of several identical items, the egg stand seemed to fit the bill perfectly. Why did he design an egg stand with seven positions, rather than say six, or twelve? Eric has it all figured out. When he's down to his last egg, he sits it in the central position, and then buys in half a dozen fresh ones. An egg stand, an *aide-mémoire* and a stimulating woodturning project, what could be better?

LATHE TYPE
A home made lathe with a $\frac{1}{2}$ HP motor and various chuck types and attachments.

TOOLS AND MATERIALS
bandsaw
$\frac{1}{2}$ in bowl gouge
$\frac{1}{2}$ in spindle gouge
round nosed scraper
1 in skew chisel
$\frac{1}{8}$ in parting tool
Craftlax Melamine
compass
workout paper
measure
and all the more general workshop tools and materials

WOOD
Various mahogany off-cuts.

What to do

1 First have a look at the photograph and the working drawings and see how the seven little holders are spigotted and glued into the base. See the crisp, clean-cut lines of the dish/tray, and note also the hexamerous placing of the egg holders.

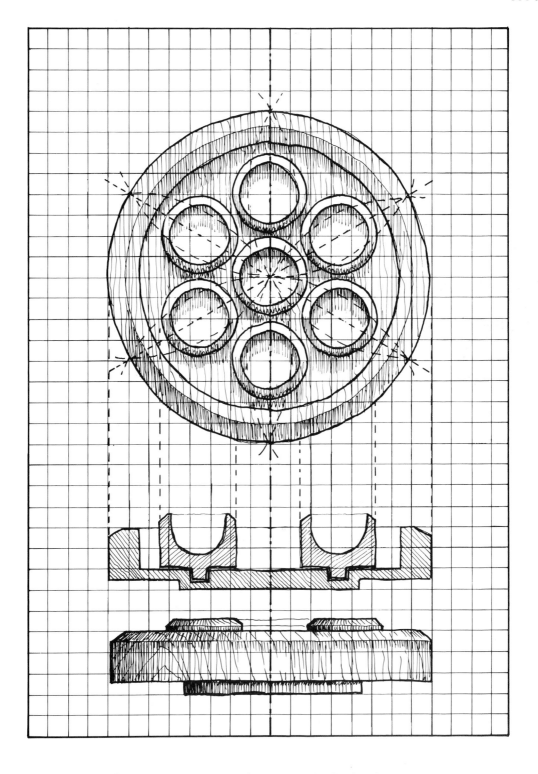

1 Working drawings. The scale is 2 grid squares to 1 in. Note how the seven egg cups/holders are set out hexagonally, and see how the spigot holes need to be kept well within the diameter of the foot.

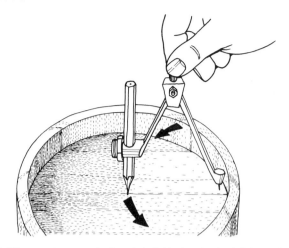

2 When you have turned off a nicely finished angle-edged dish, set the compass to the dish's radius. Then step off round the inside of the rim striking off radius arcs. Draw lines from the centre to the arc/circumference points, and fix the position of the spigot holes on these lines.

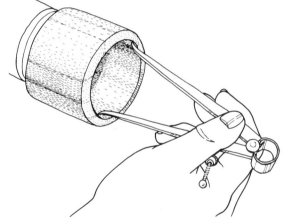

3 Use a card template and callipers to achieve seven cupped forms.

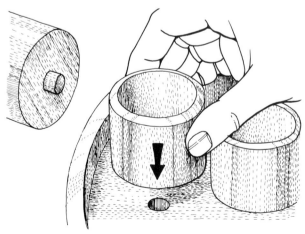

4 When you have taken the whole project to a well worked finish, dab a little glue on the spigots and set them in position.

2 Mark up the wood for the base with a compass and measure. Cut out an oversized blank on the bandsaw then mount the blank onto the lathe and true up the bottom face. Remove the blank and reposition at back onto the lathe and finish turn the piece to form the angular, stepped, dished and mitre-edged form.

3 Take the wood to a good finish, set the compass to the dish radius and then step round the circumference/rim, striking off arcs.

4 Note the size of the egg holders, and the diameter of the foot, then establish the position of the seven spigot holes.

5 Select the chuck of your choice, take the egg holder blanks, a piece at a time, and turn off the seven little cupped and spigotted forms.

6 Use callipers and cardboard templates to achieve seven identical, nicely cupped and finished holders.

7 Use a $\frac{3}{8}$ in drill bit to work the seven $\frac{1}{4}$ in deep spigot holes.

8 Finally, check that all is correct, clear the workbench of all dust and clutter, and then glue-mount the seven spigotted egg holders in their alloted holes.

Afterthoughts and modifications

At the initial pre-lathe stage this project needs to be carefully planned and marked out. To this end spend time making well considered working drawings and templates.

Use a compass set at the radius measurement to achieve the egg holder placings.

This project might perhaps be modified so that the holders double up as removable egg cups.

The placing and depth of the spigot holes in relationship to the base foot is critical. Note this point at the initial design stage.

When you are turning off the egg holders, make perhaps eight, nine, or even more, and then choose the best seven.

PICTURE AND MIRROR FRAMES

John Ernest Rhys

John Ernest Rhys, has for the last 20 or so years earned his living as a lecturer in an agricultural college. Ever since he was young he has enjoyed working with wood, and over the years, he has built, among other things, two wooden boats and a third is now awaiting completion. He is fortunate in having a large workshop of over 800 sq ft, as well as an additional storage for timber. John rarely buys new wood, but maintains a steady supply of quality wood by keeping an eye open for liquidation sales. Then again, when a suitable tree comes his way, he is able to convert the timber with his 30 in chainsaw with its very useful planking attachment.

John's approach to designing is pretty straightforward and pragmatic. First he uses odd scraps to knock up a prototype and then when he has established a rough idea of what is required, he follows through with sketches and measured drawings. Finally, when he feels that he has come to grips with all the problems and knows what he is about, he either goes back to the lathe with a piece of choice wood and turns off the project, or he drops the try-out into the scrap box.

The idea for this particular project came from his family. His wife and sister-in-law are keen tapestry workers and so he is always being asked to turn decorative hangers for bell pulls and things like that. John reckons that probably the picture frames are, in form, design and technique, a natural and logical follow-on from this work.

LATHE TYPE
Coronet Major with a 1 HP motor, a 30 in bed, a $\frac{1}{2}$ in four-prong driving centre, a $\frac{1}{2}$ in ring tail centre and a screw chuck.

TOOLS AND MATERIALS
For this project you need a tool or machine to cut a rebate (John uses a rise and fall circular saw)

1 in roughing out gouge
$\frac{1}{4}$ in skew chisel
$\frac{1}{8}$ in parting tool
$\frac{3}{8}$ in spindle gouge
callipers
tri-square
$\frac{3}{8}$ in drill bit (ideally spur point)
hand drill
Danish oil
pencil
measure
workout paper
and all the usual tools and materials

1 Working drawings. The scale is 4 grid squares to 1 in. Note the section details and the spigot-fixing of frame sides to corners. When you are marking out and cutting your wood, don't forget to allow for the spigots and lathe waste.

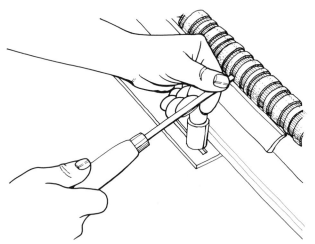

2 Cut a ½ × ½ in rebate, fix a filler piece in the rebate with double-sided sticky tape, secure the wood between centres and turn off the grooved and beaded profile.

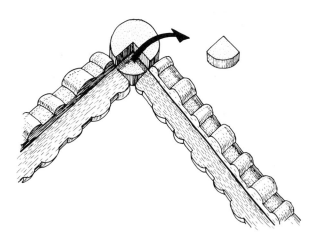

4 When the glue is dry, quarter the corner turnings and cut away the rebate-to-corner waste.

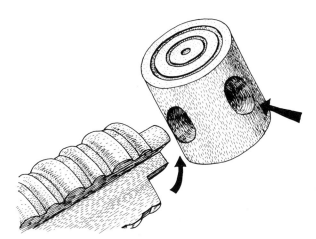

3 Bore two ⅜ in diameter, ½ in deep holes in each of the corner turnings, check that they are at right angles to each other, then glue the sides to corners.

WOODS

Four pieces of $1\frac{1}{8} \times 1\frac{1}{8}$ in square section timber of a length to suit your particular frame and four pieces of $1\frac{1}{8} \times 1\frac{1}{8} \times 2$ ins square section for the corner pieces.

What to do

1 Have a look at the working drawings and see how the sides of the frame have been spigotted into 1 in diameter corner pieces, note also the frame section and rebate.

2 Cut your prepared timber to size and then with a rise and fall circular saw (or the tool of your choice), work a $\frac{1}{2} \times \frac{1}{2}$ in rebate.

3 Using double-sided adhesive tape and a $\frac{1}{2} \times \frac{1}{2}$ in square section filler, mount the wood between suitable centres. Note: as this project is based on split turnings you might use a $\frac{1}{2}$ four-prong driving centre and a $\frac{1}{2}$ in ring tail centre, or one of the special multi chucks.

4 A piece at a time, turn the wood to size, and then cut the various necks and swelling that characterize the project.

5 Once you have established the form and length of the turnings, cut $\frac{3}{8}$ in diameter end spigots, and part off.

6 Set the four frame lengths out on the workbench, check with your measured working drawing that all is correct, and then mark out the wood for the corner pieces.

7 Mount the square section timber between centres and turn off four identical 1 in diameter, 1 in long corner pieces, giving each of the pieces an identically decorated face.

8 When you have achieved the eight turnings that make up the project (two short frame sides, two long frame sides and the four identical corner pieces), and you have taken all the wood to a good finish, clear the work bench of all clutter and set out your tools.

9 Mark out the four corner turnings and then, piece at a time, bore two $\frac{3}{8}$ in diameter, $\frac{1}{2}$ in deep holes. Have a look at the working drawings and note the placing of the holes and how they are at right angles to each other.

10 Set out the frame, check that all the spigots are well placed, make absolutely sure that the corner angles are square, check that both diagonals are the same length and then glue and clamp.

11 When the glue is dry, place the frame face down on the workbench, and then, with the tools of your choice, quarter the corner pieces and cut away the wood so that the frame rebates meet at right angles. Rub down and make good, so that the glass, picture and backing card are a comfortable fit.

12 Finally, oil and burnish the wood, cut a backing board and the job is done.

Afterthoughts and modifications

As the project stands, the rebate filler pieces are wasted. You might re-design the project slightly so that the filler pieces can be used as additional frame embellishment.

At the design stage you might visit a museum with 17th-, 18th- and 19th-century turned frames and fittings. Study particularly Jacobean split turnings and frames.

WALKING STICK TOP

Brian Smith

Brian has always enjoyed woodwork, even at school it was his favourite subject. A mahogany and oak fruit bowl, made during these formative years, still holds pride of place on his sister's dining room table. On leaving school he became an apprenticed joiner with a local brewery firm. About eight years ago when he bought a Black and Decker lathe attachment, his interest in turning really took off. Certainly, in some ways, Brian found this piece of equipment a bit restricting, but it was on this lathe that he made his early works and learnt about basic tool usage and chucking methods. And of course it didn't stop there, very soon Brian's garage was bulging with all manner of woodworking gear, a bandsaw, various hand tools, and then a Peerless $\frac{1}{2}$ HP lathe with a 4 ft bed, a turning diameter of 16 ins, 4 pulleys and 2 speeds.

Sadly, because of poor health, he had to retire, but this didn't put a stop to his woodworking activities. Brian still struggles on, through good days and bad, to do his own thing. 'My workshop is the most important thing in my life. It is a fascinating hobby.'

LATHE TYPE
A Peerless with a $\frac{1}{2}$ HP induction motor, a 4 ft bed, a max turning diameter of 16 ins, four pulleys and two speeds, dated 1980.

TOOLS AND MATERIALS
small skew chisel
small narrow-gauge round nosed scraper
workout paper
pencil
measure
various small workshop tools

Craft Lac Cellulose
Bri-Wax (clear)
Brasso or car chrome cleaner
car-care rubbing down paste
glue
plastic padding

WOODS
Small off-cut of Brazilian mahogany, and a very small piece of walnut. Note: for this project you will also need a length of beef marrow-bone and of course the walking stick.

What to do
1 First of all look at the photograph and the working drawings and see how the various turned and non-turned parts are put together. Notice how the mahogany is plugged and fixed into the bone and capped with a walnut boss.

2 Take the marrow bone, feed the nourishing contents to your dog or cat, then boil, wash and rinse and leave it out in the sun to weather.

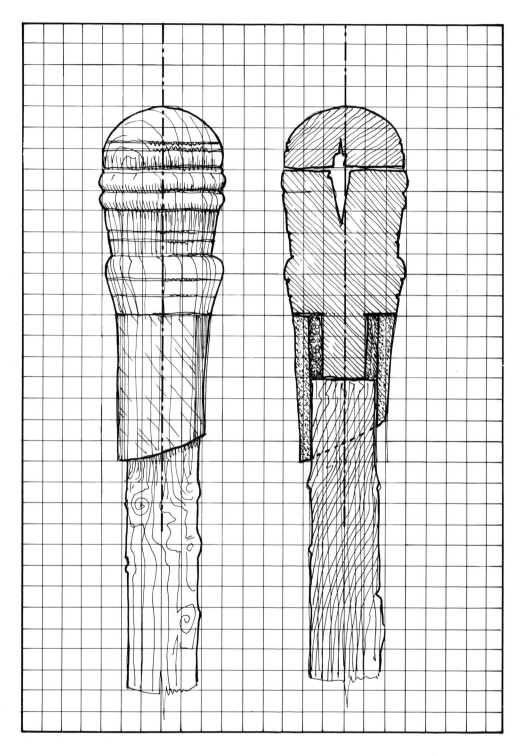

1 Working drawings. The scale is approx. 4 grid squares to 1 in. Note how the whole project has been turned and worked on a simple screw chuck. The main body of the handle is spigotted into the bone and fixed while the screw hole is concealed with a domed cap.

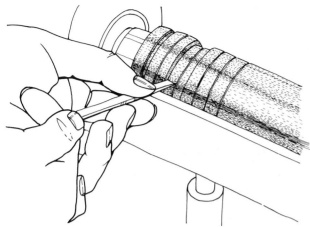

2 Secure the wood and then with the tools of your choice, turn off a plump, fist-sized, handle and take the wood to a good finish.

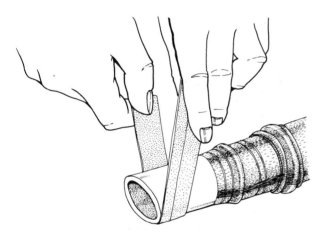

3 Glue the handle spigot, slide the bone into position, wait for the glue to dry and then work both the bone and the wood so that they run together as a single, well considered, whole.

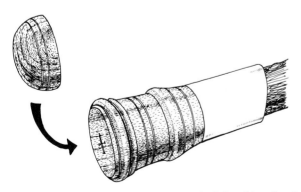

4 Fit the handle onto your chosen stick or cane, check that all is well, and finally cover the chuck hole with a domed cap.

3 Take the small piece of mahogany, mount it on the screw chuck and then with measure, callipers and the tools of your choice, turn off a nicely ringed and grooved form.

4 Measure the bone hollow, then turn off the mahogany to give it a suitably tight-fitting spigot.

5 Take the mahogany to a good size and finish, square off one end of the marrow bone, then fit, fix and pack with plastic padding.

6 Return the unit to the lathe and very carefully turn off the bone so that its profile runs smoothly into the mahogany turning.

7 Work the bone with a graded selection of glasspapers and then bring the whole to a good finish with metal polish.

8 Mount, fix and glue the bone and mahogany handle on to the walking stick and put it to one side until the glue sets.

9 Take the small piece of walnut, mount it on the screw chuck, and then turn off a little domed and grooved cap. Take the cap to a good size and finish.

10 Finally, rub down both the mahogany and walnut so that they come together and fit. Check that the chuck-screw holes are covered, then fix with glue.

Afterthoughts and modifications

It might be better to fix and plug the mahogany turning into the bone with a two-part resin glue.

The three units that make up the handle, the mahogany, the walnut and the bone, could be turned as one, although this requires a great deal of pre-lathe preparation.

The bone could be squared, temporarily plugged and then mounted on a screw chuck and turned.

The bone shank might be turned, fretted and pierced to form a decorative feature. Examples of 19th-century Japanese and Chinese bone work can be found in many museums.

PENCIL BOX

Paul Richard Swabey

Paul is certainly a hard worker. When he is not burning the midnight oil studying for his examinations, he is shut away in his 12 × 8 ft garden shed workshop, designing, making mock-ups, evaluating his design roughs and woodturning. For Paul, the most enjoyable part of turning is to see the relatively uninteresting blocks of wood become beautiful, pleasing and functional items.

Surrounded by various large and small pieces of equipment, everything from a bandsaw and power drill, through to his Arundel J4 Mk II $\frac{3}{4}$ HP lathe, Paul always starts a new piece by first playing around with ideas. He begins with a few sketches. In the case of complicated projects he may also make plasticine and clay maquettes or perhaps a prototype in deal. After that he goes straight in and starts turning. If it does not go right the first time around, he is not too bothered, because at the end of the day he reckons that it is the 'feel' and character of the wood that shapes the project.

Paul particularly enjoys making tongue-in-cheek items, such as this pencil case in the form of a pencil. The making of this project was a challenge because it involved a complicated series of processes and mock-ups before he got it just right. Paul would eventually like to establish himself as a freelance woodworker producing furniture and small items. He seems to have made a good start!

LATHE TYPE
Arundel J4 Mk II with a $\frac{3}{4}$ HP motor and a $4\frac{1}{2}$ in swing.

TOOLS AND MATERIALS
$\frac{1}{2}$ in spindle gouge
skew chisel
1 in sawtooth bit
carving gouge
bandsaw
small quantity of white polish
beeswax
wood glue
small toothed saw
and the use of a clamp and bench vice.

WOODS
Two pieces of prepared yew about 12 × $1\frac{1}{2}$ × 3 ins, a scrap of dark exotic wood for the 'lead', and a couple of deal waster blocks for the turning points. Note: For reasons of economy this project uses small glued-up pieces of wood.

What to do

1 Look at the photograph on page 23. Glue the two pieces of yew wood together to make a block that measures about 12 × 3 × 3 ins.

2 Glue the two deal waster pieces to the end of the yew so that you have a total wood length of about 16 ins.

3 Have a look at the working drawings, mark out the depth of the lid, and then run the wood through the bandsaw to separate the lid from the base.

4 Put the wood back together using a paper-and-glue filler, and secure the lid to base with a couple of woodscrews, as illustrated.

5 When the glue is dry, put the wood between centres and turn off a 2 in diameter cylinder blank.

6 Have a good look at the working drawings, and then with a ruler, pencil and callipers set out the wood and establish the guide lines.

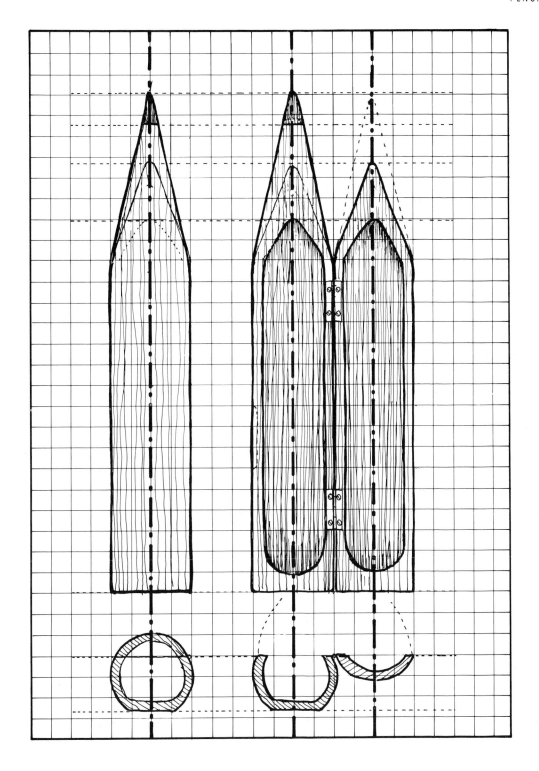

1 Working drawings. The scale is 2 grid squares to 1 in. Note the direction of the grain, the level of the lid kerf, the hinge fixing and the dark hardwood 'lead'.

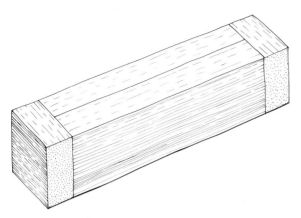

2 Build, glue and clamp the various yew and waster pieces. Aim to make a block that measures about 16 × 3 × 3 ins.

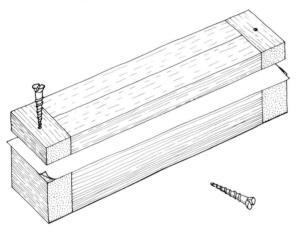

3 Cut through the block at the lid/base line, and then screw the two pieces back together using a glue-and-paper filler.

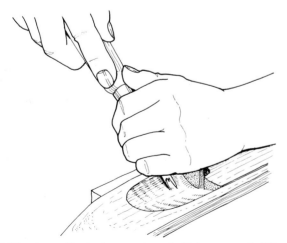

4 When the pencil box has been turned, use a flat blade to separate the lid from the base, then gouge work the interior, establish the depth of the hollow by drilling pilot holes, and remove the waste with small scoop cuts.

7 With a gouge and skew chisel, turn off the wood to achieve the gently sloping pencil box form.

8 When you have turned what you consider to be a good form, work the wood to a good finish and then take it off the lathe.

9 Using a thin, flat-bladed knife or chisel, and working with great care, part the lid from the base, then with sandpaper remove all traces of paper and glue.

10 Clamp the turned form, block at a time, in the vice, then with the sawtooth bit and gouge, work the smooth-ended hollows that make up the inside of the box.

11 Saw off the waster from the 'lead' end of the box, then place, glue and dowel the hardwood off-cut.

12 With rasp and sandpaper, rub down the hardwood 'lead' so that its contours run smoothly into the main form.

13 Cut off the other waster, rub down, seal the grain, remove all dust and then polish and wax.

14 Finally hinge the lid to the base, and cut the little box-edge thumb chamfer.

Afterthoughts and modifications

If economy is not a design factor, then the box and end wasters can be turned from a single piece of wood.

This project need not be turned between centres, you could use a special chuck.

The dark hardwood 'lead' could be built into the main block of wood at the pre-lathe preparation stage, this would make for an easier-to-work, smoother finish.

If you do decide to build-up using small scraps and off-cuts, then you might consider the use of coloured thin veneers as an additional design feature.

PHONE TABLE LIGHTER

Kenneth Harold Williams

Rustic furniture maker, fencing contractor, tree feller and woodsman, Ken Williams is also a keen carver and turner. He first started working with wood when, like a great many romantic Welshmen before him, he tried his hand at whittling a set of love spoons. His beloved (now his wife and the mother of their two year old daughter), encouraged him in his work, and he went on to make toys and then to try his hand at woodturning. His workshop, is very small, so small in fact, that before his 1 HP James Innes lath would fit in, he had to cut a bit off the lathe bed. But no matter, Ken's ambition is to have a workshop large enough to take a large cast-iron lathe that he has in store.

His wood supply presents no problem, as it is a by-product of his trade. The very wood that he used for this project, comes from a beech tree that he cut down in Colwyn Bay. Although the tree was rotten at the base, Ken saw that the bulk of the timber could be saved. By-and-by, the tree was felled, the wood was converted with his large circular saw, and then the sawn planks were left for three years to season. Ken's inspiration for the project is clear, he simply wanted to make a useful object and the table lighter seemed to fit the bill perfectly. Man of the trees, Welsh love-spoon carver, and now a wood turner, Ken is extremely enthusiastic. In fact, he now wants to go on and make a series of telephones in different woods. What else to say, except best of luck, we all hope that your ambitions are realized.

LATHE TYPE
1 HP James Innes cast iron lathe with a 'V'-pulley and four speeds.

TOOLS AND MATERIALS
1 in Robert Sorby roughing gouge
1 in skew chisel
$\frac{1}{4}$ in parting tool
three spindle gouges, $\frac{1}{4}$ in, $\frac{1}{2}$ in and $\frac{3}{8}$ in
hand drill and bits
coping saw
sanding sealer
Speed'n'eze
workout paper
pencil
measure
callipers
table lighter inset
wire wool
glass paper
and all the usual workshop tools

WOOD
Several small beech off-cuts.

What to do

1 Have a close look at the photograph on page 18 and the working drawings, and see how the project has been made up in five turned parts, a base, a stem or a central column, an ear-piece, a mouth-piece, and a sprung ear-piece clip.

2 Working between centres, turn off the main central column and the mouth-piece. Try to achieve forms that have nicely rounded beads and crisp grooves.

3 Work the central column so that it has a shoulder and spigot at one end, and a many-stepped taper at the other.

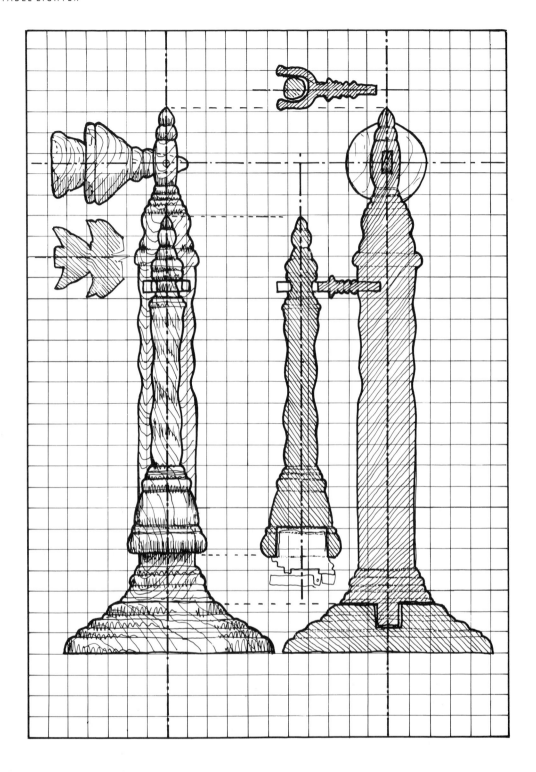

1 Working drawings. The scale is 2 grid squares to 1 in. See how the 'phone is made from five turnings. All the parts are pretty straightforward, except the ear-piece clip so it might be wise to make a prototype.

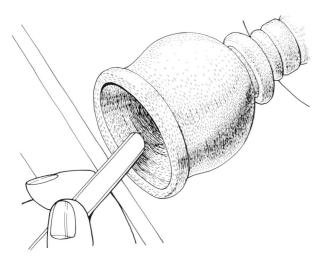

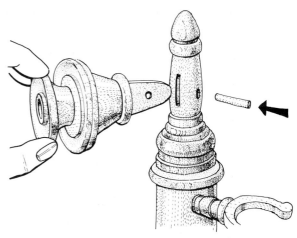

2 When you come to making the ear-piece clip, turn off a little acorn form. The inside diameter of the acorn should relate to the diameter of the ear-piece neck (see the working drawings).

4 When you are fitting the mouth-piece, cut a mortice through the top of the central column, then drill and peg.

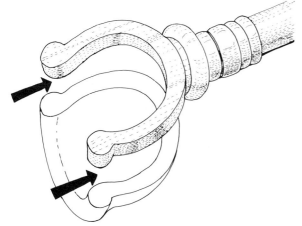

3 When you have turned off a little acorn-shaped bowl or cup, note the direction of the grain, then take a coping saw and cut away the sides so that you are left with a sprung horseshoe cross-section.

7 Turn off all the little dishes and hollows that characterize the piece.

8 Now, still working between centres, turn off the slender mace-shaped ear-piece. Note the recess for the lighter, and the necked handle at the clip point.

9 The clip can be made on a spigot chuck or one of the other specials. With callipers and your finest tools, turn off a little hollow acorn-shaped form.

10 When you have turned off all the pieces and taken them to a good finish, clear the workbench and set out your tools.

11 Fit and glue the column spigot in the base, use a coping saw to cut and work the shoulders of the mouth-piece and cut away the bowl of the little 'acorn' to make the clip.

12 Drill the central column just below the main beaded shoulder and fit the ear-piece clip. Check that the clip is well aligned.

13 Establish the position of the mouth-piece, then with a drill and chisel, cut a mortice through the top of the central column, shape both the shoulders of the mouth-piece and the

4 When you have achieved what you consider to be a good, bold column, screw the base blank to a face plate and then set about turning off the grooved and beaded disc.

5 Cut a mortice hole to fit the column spigot.

6 Mount a small scrap of wood between centres, and turn off the small cone-shaped unit which is the mouth-piece.

mortice, so that they are a good fit, and then drill and peg.

14 Drill and mortice the ear-piece and fit the lighter.

15 Finally, go over the whole project trimming up, polishing, checking alignment and generally making good.

Afterthoughts and modifications

This project is rather tricky because having turned the various pieces, they then need to be worked. To assist this process it is important that you make working drawings, detailed drawings and prototypes.

When you have turned off the little acorn-shaped ear-piece clip, note the direction of the grain before you cut away the bowl.

The lighter recess at the end of the ear-piece might better be worked on the lathe using a spigot chuck or a three-jaw chuck.

The mouth-piece needs to be fitted and pegged so that it is a firm but adjustable fit in the column mortice.

DRESSING TABLE SET

Cyril Edward Walker-Smith

The question of what to do in retirement after 48 years spent in the Aerospace industry was no problem for Cyril. With no more ado, he built himself a 20 ft long workshop and then bought a Shopsmith 'V' $1\frac{1}{2}$ HP lathe. He had always had a 'feel' for shaping wood, both for decorative and functional use, and so in no time he was creating useful, quality-finish, turned items. Woodturning has become for Cyril more than a time-filling hobby, it is an outlet for his love and appreciation of all things that are pleasing to the eye.

This self-taught craftsman is initially inspired by classical Greek motifs, then as each turned item begins to take shape, he finds the innate qualities within the wood—grain, colour and character, suggest form and design adjustments. This particular project is a one-off that was specially designed to keep his wife's costume jewellery neat, tidy and on view. As for wood, Cyril has never bought new, and in this instance he used off-cuts from a local double-glazing company.

LATHE TYPE
Shopsmith 'V' equipped with a 10 in sanding disc.

TOOLS AND MATERIALS
Standard $\frac{1}{2}$ in gouge
$\frac{1}{2}$ in and $\frac{5}{8}$ in skew
$\frac{3}{8}$ in bull nosed radius tool (home made)
$\frac{1}{4}$ in parting tool
set of miniature turning tools
lightly stained button polish
wax
you will also need all the usual workshop items

measure
callipers
pencils
paper
sandpaper
PVA glue

WOOD
Tight, smooth grained mahogany.

What to do

1 First have a good long look at the working drawings and the photograph on page 11. Note the size and shape of the various lidded containers, and how the delicate spindles spring out from the main central column, then sit down with a pencil and paper and make your own design, form and technical adjustments.

2 Set your $1\frac{1}{2}$–2 in square, 12 in long piece of prepared wood between centres and turn off a blank for the main column cylinder.

3 With one eye on the measured drawings, take calliper readings and then carefully turn the various necks, swellings and grooves that go to make up the decorative central column.

4 Look at the working drawings and see at what angle the delicate spindle-pegs spring out from the column. Note the spiral placing of the pegs and the flush peg-to-column fitting.

5 Turn, work and finish the six pegs, then with a hand drill and PVA glue, angle and set them according to your design specifications.

6 Then start work on the lidded bowls. Set out

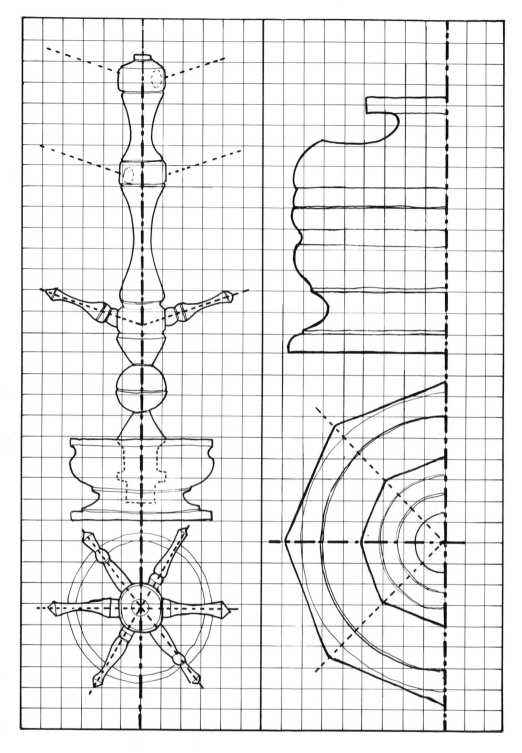

1 Working drawings. Left: the scale is 2 grid squares to 1 in. Right: the scale is 4 grid squares to 1 in. Note the fitting of column to base, the angle of pegs to central column, the 60° spiral setting of the pegs and the octagonal lid and base detail.

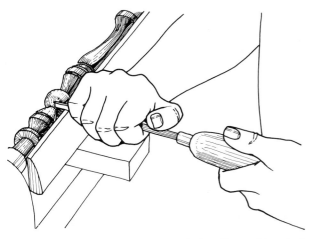

2 Turn the central column between centres and using callipers and the tools of your choice, work the various necks and swellings.

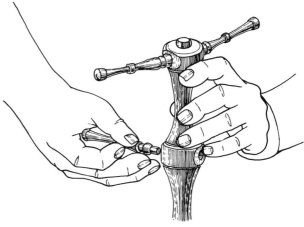

4 Set out the central column, angle and drill the peg holes and finally glue and make good.

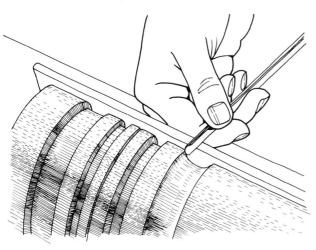

3 Turn the bowl base and lid from one piece of wood, establish the outside profile and then split and separate lid from base.

and prepare all the $3 \times 3 \times 3\frac{1}{2}$ in blocks of wood, select one and then mount it on the face place or screw chuck.

7 Turn the outside profile of lid and base, groove, split and separate lid from base. Complete the base interior and then finalize the delicate contours of lip and rim.

8 Remove the base from the face plate, mount a softwood waster and then turn a hole to receive the lid.

9 Check that the lid is a good secure friction-fit

within the hole, and then turn off the lid interior and rim.

10 When all is correct as described, take a chisel, saw, or tool of your choice, and trim both base and lid knob so that they are octagonal in form (see the working drawing plan view).

11 Sand down, lightly stain, remove all dust and lathe waste and then wax to a good finish.

12 Finally, turn off a set of well matched bowls and lids, mark off and drill for the central column, glue, put together and make good.

Afterthoughts and modifications

The angle of drill entry and placing of the pegs was something of a problem. This part of the project could have been simplified and worked with a pre-set jig- and hole-guide.

Making a matched and sized set of bowls/dishes can be tricky. It might have been simpler to give each turned form its own individual characteristics and link them by having similar design features, such as the same knobs. Cyril decided to turn the bowls so that they appeared identical, but the interiors are subtly different due to the nature of the lid fittings. One bowl has a plug fit while the other is fitted radius to radius.

DICE SHAKER

Frederick T. Ward

Fred started woodworking 11 years ago when he married Sheila. His wife is extremely artistic and pursues such diverse activities as painting, etching, embroidery and dressmaking. Such creativity inspired Fred to start woodwork. Working as a busy London taxi cab driver he didn't have much free time but as the weeks and months rolled past he found that he had made a considerable number of items—tables, cabinets, shelves, etc. Just when he was beginning to run out of new ideas Fred discovered the craft of woodturning and he hasn't looked back. An extremely creative couple, Fred and Sheila spend their time making much appreciated art and craft items for family and friends.

Fred is now retired and has more time to devote to his craft. He goes to woodworking shows, searches around for exotic wood, spends more time in his small workshop making miniatures but most importantly has time to experiment with new ideas and techniques. Sheila turns a blind eye to the rising tide of shavings and wood dust and is getting used to having Fred at home all day. Fred's retirement looks altogether enviable.

LATHE TYPE
An Arundel K450 with a $\frac{1}{2}$ HP motor, a 4 in three jaw chuck and a Precision Combination chuck.

TOOLS AND MATERIALS
selection of Sorby and Ashley Isles woodturning tools
band saw
selection of clamps
pencil
measure
workout paper
callipers
wood glue
wax
polish
all the usual workshop items

WOODS
For this project you need, a quantity of sapele and two small off-cuts of a good quality $\frac{1}{4}$ in thick, multi–layer plywood, Fred uses five-ply.

What to do

1 Look at the photograph on page 23 and the working drawings and see how the pre-lathe work involves the use of glue, clamps, a clamping box-trough and two plywood interlayers.

2 When you have considered all the implications of the project, sit down with a pencil and sketch pad and see how you might adjust and modify this project to suit your own wood turning needs. For example, you might use thin veneers or sheets of plastic or metal instead of plywood.

3 Set out your prepared wood, decide on the position and placing of the plywood interlayers and then cut and work the wood accordingly.

4 Take all the 'sandwich' faces to a good finish, then dust, glue and clamp up. Note: clamping angle-cut wood is a bit tricky, the wood tends to slip and slide about (see how Fred uses a clamping box or trough).

5 When the glue has cured, remove the box and

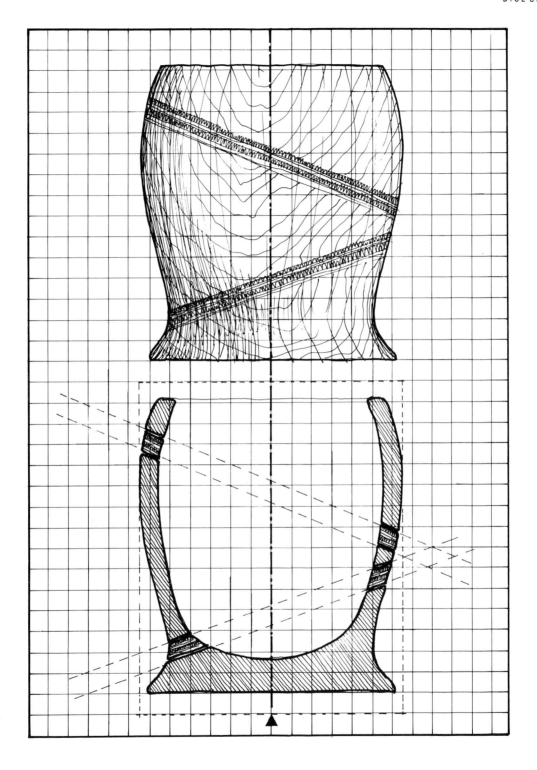

1 Working drawings. The scale is 4 grid squares to 1 in. Note how, at the pre-lathe stage, pieces of choice, fine grade multi-core plywood are glued and sandwiched into the wood to be turned.

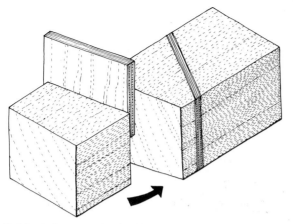

2 Select both your wood and multi-core plywood with care, then plan, cut, place and sandwich the ply so that after turning it will be seen to best effect. Note: if you can't visualize the project, turn off a prototype.

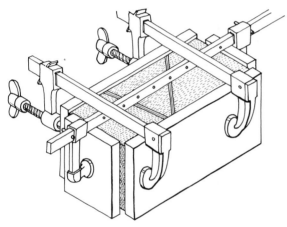

3 Set out your clamping box, or just use four pieces of wood, then dust the surfaces to be glued, then glue and clamp up.

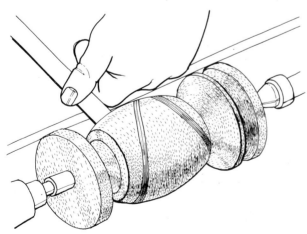

4 Finally turn the wood between centres (or use a chuck of your choice), then hollow turn. Take the wood to a good finish and part off.

clamps, clean off the working faces, and then mount the wood between centres.

6 Check that the wood is secure, then with the tools of your choice, turn the wood between centres and work the outer profile.

7 When you have achieved what you consider to be a well worked, tight form, take the wood to a good finish and part off.

8 Now mount the wood on the lathe using a screw chuck, a three jaw chuck or whatever and hollow turn to achieve a nicely considered form.

9 Finally, take the wood to a smooth polished finish, remove the wood from the lathe, make good any chuck marks and then the job is done.

Afterthoughts and modifications

By cutting, gluing, inserting interlayers, clamping up, waiting for the glue to dry and then repeating the procedure, you might work a crossed over, many layered effect. Many ethnic woodturners use thin layers of brass to achieve fine 'inlay' designs. Excellent examples can be seen in 19th-century Indian woodturning.

The pre-lathe preparation needs to be well managed. To this end, spend time making a clamping trough and planning the working sequence.

If you decide to use plywood for the interlayers, make sure you use good quality, multilayer fine ply, avoiding poor grade, thick core plywood.

At the gluing and clamping stage, make sure that all the surfaces to be glued are clean and free from dust.

Some brightly coloured woods bleed when they are sandwiched between white woods, you might use this effect in your design.